Winning Teachers

PATRICIA J. MUNSON

WITH A FOREWORD BY
ROBERT W. REASONER

Teaching Winners

ETR ASSOCIATES

SANTA CRUZ, CALIFORNIA

1991

ETR Associates (Education, Training and Research) is a nonprofit organization committed to fostering the health, well-being and cultural diversity of individuals, families, schools and communities. The publishing program of ETR Associates provides books and materials that seek to empower young people and adults with the skills to make positive health choices. We invite health professionals to learn more about our high-quality resources and our training and research programs by contacting us at P.O. Box 1830, Santa Cruz, CA 95061-1830.

The following educators contributed to the development of this book:

Sue Myers, Superintendent
Strawberry Pine School District
Pine, Arizona

Karen Mitchell-Wichelmann,
    Teacher
San Lorenzo Valley Elementary
    School
Felton, California

Andrea Seitz, Director of
    Curriculum
Live Oak School District
Santa Cruz, California

Verna McDonald, Special Education
    Teacher
Slonaker Elementary School
San Jose, California

10 9 8 7 6 5 4 3 2

Printed in the United States of America

Cover design by John Simon
Text design by Julia Chiapella

Library of Congress Cataloging-in-Publication Data

Munson, Patricia J.
        Winning teachers, teaching winners / Patricia J. Munson.
        p.   cm.
    ISBN 1-56071-058-6
        1. Teachers—Professional ethics—United States. 2. Self-respect.
    3. Integrity 4. Teaching.   I. Title.
    LB17779.M86   1991
    174'.9372—dc20   91-3244

Title No. 593

To Grama June, she believed in me.

April 11, 1992

Dearest Talea and Tim,

The very best always

~

Namaste

I love you!

Patricia Munson

Dimensions In Discovery
Patricia J. Munson-Holladay
984 South Cypress Ave.
San Jose, CA 95117
(408) 261-9727

Contents

Foreword

A major concern of the education community today is how to implement the reforms and restructuring required to match the needs of our changing world. Almost every education and business journal one picks up addresses the nature of the restructuring that should take place. Yet, it is rare when one of these journals addresses the key element in school change—the mental health of the teacher and staff.

The nature of the reforms being proposed today cannot be legislated or mandated by government edict, school boards or superintendents, for today the keys to effective education lie in initiative, commitment, compassion and dedication to children. These essential qualities depend upon how teachers feel about themselves.

Patricia Munson answers the question of why some schools are ineffective and unchanged, while other schools bubble with enthusiasm, innovation and excitement. She finds that the answer lies in the ability of staff members to communicate effectively and to form healthy, supportive relationships with each other.

It has been my experience that she is exactly correct. As educators, we must look at our own sense of worthiness and level of self-esteem. We cannot expect to implement change or assist in elevating the self-esteem of our students if, by example, we have chosen isolation, cynicism and discouragement for ourselves.

We know that approximately one-third of our teachers today suffer from low self-esteem to the point where it cripples their effectiveness with students. When teachers feel inadequate, unappreciated and isolated, they become more punitive in their actions, display less patience in their instruction, demonstrate less compassion for students and engage in less effective problem solving. The results are reflected in students who see school as an uncaring institution, who lack motivation, who see little point in continuing in school and who engage in deviant behavior to compensate for their own feelings of inadequacy.

How teachers feel about themselves is obviously the key to effective change in the schools. Munson is one of the few to recognize that critical need and to prepare materials for the teaching professional. With her background and her practical, no-nonsense approach, she has been able to combine the concepts of motivation and personal effectiveness with the sound practices of mental health to provide an outstanding source of practical ideas, suggestions and prescriptions for developing teacher self-esteem. She has done an outstanding job of sharing her vision of how things can be and of illustrating the concepts through the use of everyday classroom experiences.

The material in this book addresses how we can go about changing ourselves to work with others in more productive ways—with integrity so that we each grow in self-esteem and personal effectiveness. It will be of great value to all teachers and administrators having to examine the need for change and restructure to build better programs for our students of today and the citizens of tomorrow.

—ROBERT W. REASONER

Robert Reasoner served as superintendent of the Moreland School District in San Jose, California, for 11 years. Under his direction, the Moreland district became known for its outstanding schools, receiving both state and national recognition for academic excellence and the empowering climate for staff and students. Reasoner is the author of Building Self-Esteem: A Comprehensive Program for Schools, *and serves as executive director of the California Center for Self-Esteem and chair of the International Council for Self-Esteem. He has been named "National Educator of the Year" by the National Council for Self-Esteem.*

Acknowledgments

I wish to thank my children, Alan, Pamella and Jennifer; they are my greatest contribution and my most cherished teachers. My thanks to Verna McDonald, without whose support and unconditional love this would not have been possible; to Kathryn Forstmann for hundreds of hours of unconditional support; to Kathleen Middleton of ETR Associates for believing I could do this; to Thomas, who reminds me to ask for what I want; and to my parents and sisters, who love me.

Integrity
with a Capital I

"To thine own self be true." These are powerful words. When I began to explore the topic of self-esteem and self-confidence, I realized that to have a foundation on which to cultivate and support self-esteem, I had to have a sense of personal integrity. My personal definition of integrity is written throughout this book.

The issue is not whether educators have external integrity: Do they know right from wrong? Are they ethically honest? Can they be trusted not to steal? The answer to these questions for educators is usually a resounding *yes*. That is not the point. The point of this offering is to examine how educators are doing in the category called internal or personal integrity—their integrity with themselves and those they interact with on a daily basis.

Personal integrity deals with how well I know myself, my

trust level with myself, my willingness to know my truth for me and express it to others in a way that supports both of us. The question is, Am I the teacher I dreamed of being, making the difference I knew I could make?

As I begin to explore my depth of personal integrity, I see a direct link between my level of integrity and my feelings of high or low self-esteem. Having high self-esteem means that I like myself—what I do, what I say, who I am and most of all, who I am becoming. It means that I hold myself in high esteem, regardless of what others may say or do, regardless of how they may feel. I know who I am and what I stand for as a human being.

For many of us, the foundations of self-esteem were not laid down in a way that supported us strongly. Many of us had parents or role models who were not confident in what they were doing or who they were. As a result, we are now exploring how to turn soggy inner foundations into more concrete platforms on which to stand.

If part of your reason for teaching is to give children a solid platform on which to stand, then it makes sense to do a little inspection of your own foundation. We cannot assist others to build a strong foundation if we are standing on a shaky one ourselves.

My definition of integrity involves feeling whole and integrated, knowing who we are and what we stand for. When we have integrity, we feel the excitement that comes from knowing we can count on ourselves to take care of ourselves and others in a way that truly supports everyone.

We function from a place of personal responsibility and

not a place of blame, shame or regret. We know that we can trust ourselves to make good and sound decisions and follow through on them. We are not swayed by somebody else wanting us to buy into their wants and desires when it may not serve us to do so.

We act on tasks and situations as soon as we see what needs to be done rather than waiting for them to change on their own or by someone else's hand. Finally, we realize that people can count on us when we know we can count on ourselves.

This is integrity—a firm foundation for cultivating self-esteem and self-confidence. When we live our lives from a place of personal integrity and hold ourselves in high esteem, we can teach our students to do the same. We cannot teach our students to be winners when we feel less than winners ourselves.

As teachers, we must demonstrate personal integrity and honesty, rooted in respect for the truth. Integrity is honesty with one's self and all others. It is recognizing that only when we consider and respect the rights of others are our own rights secure. The value of integrity is manifested in regard for others, wholesome family and community relationships, and a strong sense of responsibility for our neighbors.

In classrooms and out of them, we are all teachers. With this book, I hope to raise the level of awareness of how integrity operates in our lives, how it is reflected in the quality of life and how, without it, our lives, both as human beings and educators, cease to be all that they can be.

3

As we look at integrity for educators, we need to do a little exploring of the integrity we each have as individuals. If we want to ensure that integrity operates in the educational process, we need to understand what it is and how it operates in our personal lives.

What Does Integrity Mean to You?

If I were to ask you to define integrity, what would you say? I don't mean Webster's definition, but your personal definition. I have asked this question of hundreds of people and received some very interesting answers. For some it is "walking my talk," being true to myself and others, living my principles or simply wholeness.

Some people just look at me blankly and shake their heads. Yet, when I ask them if they know what integrity is, they say they do; they just can't define it. Think about your personal definition of integrity and how it operates in your life. You may even want to write it down.

Webster defines integrity as: (1) strict adherence to a standard of value or conduct; (2) personal honesty and independence; (3) completeness, unity; (4) soundness.

Is your definition of integrity identical to mine? What about the person next to you or the teacher in the next classroom? Is Tom's mother's sense of integrity the same as Cassandra's father's or Jose's grandmother's?

Probably not. Each of us has our own brand of integrity. Our definitions of integrity and how we choose to apply them may look very different. How did that happen and where did these definitions come from?

Why would one person never throw a piece of paper on the street and another not give it a second thought? Why would one person always return an overpayment of change at a store and another feel totally justified in keeping it? Why would one teacher go out of his or her way to personally contact every parent of every child in class, while another feels mandatory attendance at functions other than the once-a-year open house is beyond the scope of the job?

I believe integrity is based on how we were raised, who raised us, where we grew up, our culture, race, religious environment, the schools we attended, the teachers who taught us. Our life experiences shape the guidelines, the principles, the values, the *integrity*, by which we live our lives and relate to others.

It isn't up to me to decide how you define what is right or wrong. It is an individual decision. But we choose people to be close to in our lives based on the potential alignment of our integrity with theirs.

It gets too uncomfortable to be around people whose integrity is not somewhat aligned with our own. If someone wants to swear, act out in public or be just plain obnoxious, I don't get a vote about his or her behavior. But I do get a vote as to whether I want to spend time around this person or have him or her in my life to some degree.

You get to live your life any way you choose. If your integrity and mine are not aligned, that doesn't make you wrong, but I may choose not to have you closely involved in my life. If I live within my personal definition of integrity, I will choose my relationships based on this definition.

Relationships in and out of the Classroom

We are responsible for having each and every relationship with each and every student in our classroom work. Even though I might not choose to have a child or his or her parents in my personal life, I am the one who is committed to doing whatever it takes for all of us to work and learn harmoniously. Easy? Probably not. Part of my job? Yes.

When we act from a place of personal integrity, the need for assistance in student-teacher relationships from a parent, principal, psychologist or the teacher next door becomes obvious much sooner. It is also easier to ask for help. When we function from personal integrity, it is usually easier to recognize that everything that can be done has been done and that this child may need a different learning environment.

A decision based in integrity relies solidly on what is best for the child. It does not arise out of desperation over negative behaviors or a relationship that has become completely unworkable for all—student, teacher and parents. Most teachers have experienced both ways of making class changes, and we know how long it takes to recover from an unworkable scenario.

I was lecturing for a battered women's group several years ago. One young women said that the man in her life had thrown a radio at her and that was the end of the relationship. She considered that act abuse, and she packed her bags and left forever. Another woman asked if the radio had hit her. The first woman replied no, but the fact that this man had thrown it was enough for her. He had crossed the line that defined her integrity, and she would not and could not tolerate that behavior in her life.

Each of us has a line beyond which we will not go. Sometimes we move the line; but when push comes to shove, most of us have a place where we would fight to the death rather than move the line another millimeter.

As we live and grow, our integrity may change. The lines we draw around our behavior and our tolerance of other people's behavior may change. But it's important to understand how our own integrity is defined and how it affects how we live and relate to others.

I am convinced that if you are still reading at this point, you want more from the adventure of life then you are currently receiving. If this is not true, you may want to simply loan this book to a friend and go over to the couch for a nap. If I am right, then I challenge you to continue to read. As you do, seriously evaluate your teaching career and your life to see whether you are getting the greatest value and more importantly, giving the greatest value. Are you living your true integrity?

There are very few things that we can call our own in this life. One of these things is who we are and how we choose to live our lives. We are in a precarious time on our planet. If we can't take responsibility, each and every one of us, to find and live our own integrity, to take a stand for survival and teach our children what they need to know, none of us may make it.

Educators shape the lives and the minds of our children, sometimes to a greater degree than their parents. We cannot afford, as a country or as a species, not to pay committed attention to what we communicate to our children, verbally and nonverbally, as well as what we allow others to communicate to them.

As hard as it may be for you to believe, you may be the one to make the difference. Take a stand, take a risk, draw the line. If each one of us takes responsibility for our corner of the world, the world can and will change. If we all wait for someone else to do it, we will all lose. We are the someone.

Life's Decisions— Chance or Choice?

Have you ever awakened in the morning with an empty feeling? There's food in the fridge, gas in the car and a roof over your head. All should be well with the world, and yet everything seems to have a cloud over it. No matter which way you look, things look grim. There is no apparent reason for this awful feeling, and yet it persists. You seem to be in the bottom of a barrel with no way out.

I don't think there is a human being who has not had this experience. For some, unfortunately, it may be the entire experience of life; for others, an occasional day or two or month or two, here and there. We all know how it makes us feel—powerless, futile, disheartened or somewhat discouraged.

These feelings can be a message that it's time to examine our integrity with the world and the people in it, as well as our relationship to both. Life works when our relationships with ourselves and the people in our world are in good working order.

How can we go about changing these feelings of despair? I suggest we begin to examine how we are making our choices. Although the experience could have another cause, a simple place to begin and one that has worked for hundreds of my students is to be willing to look at our choices. Each of us makes hundreds and sometimes thousands of decisions a day. The first ones each day are probably, Should I open my eyes? Should I get up now? Shall I have coffee or tea?

The choices tend to get a bit more challenging as the day goes on. A teacher once said to me, "The number of choices and decisions a teacher must make each day is second only to the number made by an air traffic controller."

How we make these choices and how honest we are with ourselves and others about our choices affects our quality of life and how we feel about our life experience in general. The way we make these choices can cause our lives to be joy-filled and happy or to be a series of overcast, gloomy days. Let's explore four areas of choice that may get us off track and out of alignment with our personal integrity.

POINTS OF INTEGRITY

Irresponsible Choices	Responsible Choices
• I don't get a vote.	• I make all my choices.
• I feel blame, shame and regret.	• I have all my votes.
	• I am accountable.

Irresponsible Choices	Responsible Choices
• Please love me, please love me.	• I do that which I choose to do with a happy heart and not merely for another's approval.
• I fear your disapproval if I do not do what you want me to.	
• I say yes and mean no.	
• I wait for someone else to handle it.	• I act as soon as I see what needs to be done and I do it. (Postponed choice has high emotional cost.)
• I wait for something else to happen.	
• I have a good reason for every broken agreement.	• I keep agreements, or I renegotiate them to the highest benefit for all.
• I "try" to get things done.	

I Don't Get a Vote

Any time I decide that I don't get a vote about how I will live my life, I have stepped outside my personal integrity. I have become the victim of my circumstances.

Whoever I have decided *does* get the vote in my life runs my life. He made me; she made me; they made me; the government makes me; my school district makes me; my principal, my parents, my students make me. Everybody gets a vote but me.

Students love to take this tack. You may be the bane of their existence. You make them do all kinds of awful things. How would your classroom be different if your students began to realize that they do what they do because it serves them to do so—not because you make them? Students win or lose based on their own choices, and so, by the way, do you.

No one makes you or me do anything. That's right, no one. We choose to do things for a variety of reasons. We usually choose based upon what is in it for us. Sometimes we do what we do to protect what we think we will lose if we do not.

THE DOODLER

A young student refuses to use his class time effectively. He doodles, disrupts others and has to take "time out." The natural consequence is that he has to take the work home to finish. His resistance to taking the work home manifests in loud protest and much complaining.

This goes on for several days. His parents are asked to assist in getting the work completed at home. Soon, the discomfort of working with his parents outweighs the discomfort of settling down at school and getting it done.

This student begins to see that doing his work at school serves him. He has more free time at home, less hassle from his parents, and no one is giving him much attention for his loud protest or complaining. When he sees that it serves him to choose to do his work in school, he will do so.

Students feel empowered if they see that they have some choice. As they are allowed to make choices, they begin to learn which choices serve them and which do not, instead of feeling at the mercy of everyone else's choices. Students will often choose what serves them when they can see the prices they pay for the choices they make. Sometimes, we as teachers might do well to allow our students to experience natural consequences.

Some of us decide that we are the victim of someone else's decisions for us or the way or place we were raised. But the truth is that you have made every decision pertinent to where you are right now. You can have your life be what you want it to be if you want it enough.

I have worked with hundreds of socially and economically underprivileged men and women. I watch with wonder what happens in their lives when they begin to understand that they get a vote, that if they are willing to do what it takes to have what they say they want, they can have it.

All too often, we simply mouth the words. We moan about what is not happening, what we would do if only..., how it could be if it were not for..., or how it will be when such and so forth happens. The question is, How committed are we to having what we say we want, rather than blaming someone else for what we do not have or claiming to be the victim of another's choice for us or of our circumstances?

Did you go to college because your parents wanted you to go? Did you want to go? Did you go to the college of your choice or the one your mom or dad went to? Where did you live, on-campus or off-campus? Who paid for all of this?

If you went to a college your parents chose, you went because you wanted to or you would have done something else. It benefited you in some way to do so. Ask yourself honestly, could you have done something else? Why didn't you? What were the payoffs for going along? Were you truly the victim, or did you choose to give up your vote?

Who chose the school you teach in? Who chose the grade you teach?

Who chose your attitude toward your students and their parents? Who decides, day by day, what will happen in your classroom and what the standards and quality of what you teach will be? Who decides whether you will participate positively in staff meetings, sit quietly in boredom or assume the posture that what you say doesn't matter anyway?

When we choose to work in a setting that provides autocratic decision making, we need to look at how it serves us to have our decisions made for us. Note that a non-decision is also a decision, e.g., "It's OK that they gave me Grade 1, I'll manage somehow." One alternative is to choose to enjoy what you have, rather than to be victim to it. Another choice would be to find an educational setting that provides on-site inter-active decision making where you could have more input on your grade level placement.

If you don't live where you want to, if you don't drive the car you want to, if you don't wear the clothes you want to, who do you suppose is going to change it for you? Who chose these things in the first place? Everything you want is out there. Are you committed enough to go get it? If we don't have what we want, it is due less to someone who won't let us have it than to our own unwillingness to go get it.

You always have the vote in your life. Nobody else gets the vote unless you give it to them. This is always true and always will be true—to the end of your life. It may not be easy to make choices and it may take some doing, but you always have the vote.

We get into trouble when we feel powerless, as though somebody else has power over us. Our power is our own, if we choose to use it. Of course, there are prices to pay for the choices we make, but we always have choices.

I am well aware, after ten years of teaching these concepts, that there may be exceptions. I have, however, rarely seen them. I have worked with physically handicapped, emotionally handicapped and economically handicapped men, women and children; once they see they have *the vote*, their lives can take on whole new meaning. They begin to define what they want and to discover how they can get it.

Saying Yes When You Mean No

A friend and colleague pokes a head inside your classroom door on Friday after school. Your friend asks, in a cheery yet somewhat seductive way, "Hi, what are you doing?" You feel an invisible hook reach out to grab you. At a gut level, you know that what is coming is a question that involves your participation: Could you take my morning duty on Monday? Do you have $100 I can borrow until payday on Tuesday? Can you give me a ride to school next week while my car is in the shop?

I am in favor of each of us asking for what we need and want. What I am suggesting here is that, as the recipients of a request, we listen to our true feelings before we answer and that we answer from honesty and a place of true choice rather than from a desire to avoid disfavor. Sometimes we operate out of a "please love me, please love me" need, doing anything we can to hold on to another's affection or approval.

Ask yourself how many times last week you said yes when you meant no or felt no. Close your eyes and think about it. Now, ask yourself if the other person knew that you really didn't want to do whatever he or she had requested of you. On some level we know, even when we do not acknowledge it. When someone says yes and means no or says no and means yes, we have a feeling of mistrust.

Whatever you choose to do is all right; the point is how honest you and I are being with the people in our lives and, more importantly, with ourselves. I want people in my life who are honest with me and people with whom I can be honest—it saves lots of time and energy.

I want people in my life who can look inside themselves and tell me the truth when I ask them for something. I also want people in my life to whom I can tell the truth. It's a solid feeling. I don't have to make excuses, dance around searching for the right words, make up stories or, worse yet, lie.

In twenty years on the speaker's platform, I have *never* had a student tell me that she or he would rather be lied to than dealt with honestly. Some people may think they would rather be lied to, but on closer examination, they always realize that the truth is what works every time. Even if we don't necessarily like the no, an honest no beats a dishonest yes every time.

You ask to borrow my car. I cross my arms across my

chest and heave a heavy sigh of exasperation, rolling my eyes and leaving a horribly long pregnant pause between us. Eventually, in what seems hours, I say a somewhat sarcastic "sure." You know I meant no, and I know I meant no.

Now, depending on how badly you need to borrow my car, you might choose to borrow it anyway, but I can pretty much guarantee you won't feel good about it. And it may be a very long time before you ask me again.

Although you might have been somewhat upset with me for a negative reply, you would have known what I'd meant. When we tell the truth, we begin to clean up our lives. Soon communication is easier.

Not long ago, I realized that I would be out of town for an evening meeting I conduct. I called a friend and colleague and asked her to run the meeting. She was delighted; we exchanged some chatter and hung up. I have called the same person other times, when her response was that she was not available to assist with the meeting.

She and I have given ourselves permission to tell each other the truth. We know what we can count on from each other. We can request anything from one another, knowing that we do what we can when we can and that we never have to do anything that doesn't work for us.

Exceptions? Sure! There are times when I would rather lie on my bed and read a book than babysit my grandchildren. When that happens, I ask myself what I am willing to do about it. If in my heart of hearts I know I need to take care of myself or if I simply don't want to babysit, I have some choices. I can say no from the start. I can renegotiate the agreement, if I have already made it. I can say yes and choose to be happy about my choice.

The important point is that the choice is made from a place that serves both you and the person making the request. If, for example, I say yes to babysitting and I don't mean it, my children know it and so do I. Usually this brings on a series of irritating calls from them during their absence, asking if everything is all right with the grandchildren.

I have raised a number of little ones, and my children are not concerned as to whether I can care for babies. These calls are really made to find out if our relationship is all right. When I come from integrity in my choice to sit or not to sit, I rarely hear from my children from the time they leave the grandchildren to the time they return.

I work hard not to say yes when I mean no. If I say yes, I choose to be happy about my choice. We always have a choice if we choose to exercise it.

Postponed Choice

Mary Kay, the cosmetics queen, says that procrastination is suicide in installments. I agree with her. Every time we know that we should handle something and we do not, a little piece of us dies. A little piece of our self-confidence suffers; there is a little more evidence that we cannot do what we say we can or will.

The price we pay for procrastination is very high. Think about a relationship you have enjoyed in the past—one that is no longer in the form it once was, a marriage, an old friendship, an old romance. You know, someone you once were very close to and now rarely, if ever, see. Now think about when you knew the relationship was over compared to when you actually called it off.

Most of us have had the experience of knowing that it is time to leave a job or break with a sweetheart or even get a divorce, but instead of handling it, we hang in there waiting for something to happen, for someone else to handle it. Hanging out in hope that it will get better when we know darn well it won't is a downhill journey at best. Look at how much *emotional interest* we pay when we do not handle situations we know need to be handled. What a drain on our productive energy.

Procrastination can cause us to realize at the end of our journey that there is no time left to do all the things we were so sure we would do. Steven Levine, the author of *Who Dies?*, says that those who are afraid to die are those who refused to truly live. The price we pay for procrastination is enough to kill us.

Reasons or Results

One of my favorite sayings is that we have either reasons or results and reasons do not count. Our society does a lot of what I call selective listening and non-committed committing. I will be there, I will do that, you can count on me or I'll call you tomorrow can mean if nothing better, more interesting or simpler comes along.

THE APPOINTMENT

Let's pretend for a moment that I am your principal and that you need to talk with me about a new student who you believe may have some special needs that have not been evaluated. In your opinion, it is a rather important matter. You follow the proper protocol and schedule an early morning appointment with me for 7:45 a.m. the following day.

The following day you arrive at my office at 7:40 a.m., but you are told by the secretary that I have not returned from an early district meeting. You take a seat, and wait patiently—7:50, 8:00, 8:10, 8:15. You have a class at 8:30, so you stand to leave. I rush in full of apologies about running out of gas and ask you to meet with me tomorrow at 7:15 a.m. You are now running late yourself, but you agree.

The next day you arrive at my office at 7:10 a.m.; the secretary informs you that I have been called away to another part of the school and she is sure I will be right back. You take a seat—7:20, 7:30, 7:40, 7:45. You have a meeting with a parent at 8:00, and I still have not shown up. Now you would like to forget the whole thing, but you need to meet with me to get the matter resolved for your student. As you are leaving, the phone rings and it's me. I am very sorry, but I had a flat tire. I am so embarrassed. Could we meet this afternoon after school?

By the second episode, do you care about my reasons? Probably not. While you were waiting for me the first time, a knot was forming in your stomach, anxiety began to bubble up. Believe it or not, all the times you got left somewhere as a kid came back to haunt you—all the times that Mom forgot to pick you up after school, all the times a high school friend was coming by and never got there, all the times you felt let down by someone—even the times you may have waited for a principal.

Each of us has our own list of past episodes. A part of us questions whether we are valuable enough to keep commitments to in the first place, especially if we do not keep commitments to ourselves. When I don't keep my commitment to you, either, it becomes very destructive, regardless of the story or reason behind it.

Well, you say, running out of gas, a flat tire, those are pretty good excuses, aren't they? Yes, that is exactly what they are—excuses. I believe in doing whatever it takes to keep the commitment.

If I run out of gas, I am at least going to call you, so I don't leave you stranded wondering where I am. The second time, I would be willing to walk to the school on my knees to keep the commitment. Why? There are at least two very good reasons—me and you.

Whenever I break an agreement, I pay the price first. It breaks down my self-esteem, my credibility with myself, my self-trust, my self-confidence. It causes me not to be able to trust myself. If I cannot trust myself, who can I trust?

Second, and just as important, is you, the person I have

let down. From this point forward, you may never be waiting for me anywhere without worrying that I am going to leave you standing there and never show up or call, just as before. You have it on good evidence that you cannot trust me. You may even have decided that I do not care about you as an individual.

In the case of our interactions with students and parents, establishing relationships based on trust is vital. Trust is broken when we break agreements or do not do what we say we will do.

When we're on time to let students into the classroom, we let them know we expect them to be on time. When we are not on time, we give students permission to be late, in addition to breaking an agreement. In your memory you will find your own examples of projects you agreed to set up and did not, books you promised to read and did not, games you promised to play and did not.

Think about the parents and students who have this game operating in their lives—lateness, homework, lunch money.

THE HUNGRY CHILD

A student came to school angry, upset and argumentative each morning. After three days of allowing the student to try to work it out, the teacher approached him privately. The teacher discovered that the child's mother promised to make him breakfast and give him his lunch money each evening. But each morning she refused to get up, and he left the house feeling hungry, let down and uncared about.

For a little child, the embarrassment of arriving without lunch or lunch money is almost too much to bear. Children have few options available to them. The fact that this student's mother worked late night shifts ceased to be important after a while. What his experience told him was that he could not trust what he was told.

This teacher assisted the child and the mother to come to an agreement that could be kept. The teacher and the mother agreed that the boy and his mother would set out what he needed for breakfast each night before she left for work and he went to bed. The lunch money was sent in the form of a check each Friday. If it did not arrive, the teacher called the parent, and the adults worked it out.

Children need people in their lives who show them how life works best. Keeping our agreements with children teaches them to keep theirs. It also offers them a valuable lesson in trust.

Personal credibility is also at stake here. Without personal credibility, without knowing I can count on me to keep agreements with myself and others, how can I possibly believe I can create any results that will matter? My life becomes a long line of excuses and stories about why I never created the results in my life that I said I would.

The big wins in your life, and in the lives of your

students, start with keeping the little agreements. They start with establishing a high level of trust with ourselves and the people around us. They come from being able to count on ourselves and know in our deepest place that others can count on us as well.

Locus of Control

The concept of locus of control offers another way to look at living by choice or by chance. Locus of control relates to our beliefs about who or what determines our actions.

Most people come from one orientation or the other. Either we come from a place of taking internal responsibility for our actions and their causes and effects, or we see our lives as the result of external causes. One is an accountable place to come from; the other blames someone or something else.

When we compare points of integrity and look at where we make our choices from, we become accountable for our actions. We can then assist our students to begin making their choices from an internal locus of control. Students who choose from internal orientation believe in their ability to create what they want and to make it happen in their lives.

The Three Ts—
Tell the Truth, Tell the Truth,
Tell the Truth

Perhaps more now than at any other time in the history of education, our students are looking to us for the truth about who we are and who they can become. Before we can assist students, we must ask the question: How well do we know ourselves? We cannot teach our students about something we aren't at least looking at.

Before we can hope to influence children's self-esteem in a positive way, we must know what is true about our own values, belief systems and thought processes. If I try to tell you something I myself do not believe and do not own as true, at some level you will not believe me. If I do not believe something is true for me, I will not be able to communicate it as truth to you.

The front of a classroom is a powerful place to be. The responsibility is awesome. You cannot teach and empower children to be successful if you do not hold yourself to be so. Everything you are and all that you believe is transmitted to your students at some level. We owe it to our students and ourselves to be sure that who we are and what we believe is really our truth.

There are those who say that before we can teach anyone anything of value we must know it. Others say we teach what we most need to learn. I think the truth lies somewhere in between. But if we are looking at how well we know ourselves, I don't think we can ever know ourselves too well.

In 1979 what I knew about myself was that I was a mom, a wife, a teacher-facilitator, a soccer mother, a girl scout leader and someone's daughter, sister and aunt. I knew I had some skills, yet I was so busy trying to hold it all together that I really had very little idea who I was. I wasn't sure what my goals were or if I even had any. I just adopted the goals of the environment I was in rather than creating personal ones of my own.

The process of beginning to find out who I was and what I wanted became very exciting and in a positive way, also frightening. I changed my whole life's work because of that exploration. One of the things I found was that the person I had been showing people and the person I was were not one and the same.

The Patricia I showed others was efficient, well put together, not very approachable (I didn't want anyone to get too close), got the job done, and I am sorry to say, probably hurt a lot of feelings and made some people pretty angry. On the inside I knew I was this kind, sweet, loving, open and approachable human being, and I could not understand why people could not see that.

I also realized that when push came to shove, I was so busy running around doing things that I really didn't know what I wanted or how I wanted to get there. I had not told myself the truth in a very long time, and at that point, I had no idea what it was for me.

Because I did not know who I was, how I fit into the picture, how I affected others with my behavior, I was not able to communicate effectively with anyone else. Others saw a person in a whirl of activity. When I communicated with them, there was a lack of genuineness that did not allow them to really know me, because I did not really know myself. They saw the fabricated me.

This lack of communication became evident when I spoke to an assistant or attempted to train someone about enthusiasm on the job and how to help people be comfortable in their environment. I was not comfortable with myself, nor was I enthusiastic. So even though I knew what I wanted to communicate to people, it would come across with a giant thud. I couldn't figure out why others couldn't understand what I was talking about and follow my suggestions.

If an assistant had a problem and needed to speak with me, I could sense that there was an issue, but I never understood why others appeared to have such a difficult time approaching me with problems. I had no understanding of how I came across to people or what I was doing that caused people to be so uncomfortable with me in difficult situations. The time had come for me to tell myself the truth.

I had to really look at who I was and how I was affecting others. I had to work on having the person I show the world align with the person I knew I was. My communication needed to become one with the truth for me.

The role models I had growing up had a very difficult time knowing who they were. I took my lead from them, just as you did from your role models and just as your students do from you. As teachers, we influence young minds and hearts as they form their belief systems and develop their self-esteem.

How Now, Brown Cow?

To be ridiculous for a moment, let us say that we grow up being told that chocolate milk comes from brown cows. If there is never any evidence in our world to prove otherwise, it is very safe to say that we will believe that always. We have seen cows, and we know that is where milk comes from. If we've never been to a farm or milked a cow, our belief system forms around what we've been told by someone we trust—brown cows give brown milk.

A belief system is just that—a system of beliefs that we build or collect to support our points of view of how the world is. Then we go about our lives gathering evidence to support the belief system that was given to us or that we created. If we have never stopped to think about our belief system, we may be functioning from some outdated belief system bought into years ago.

How many students have come to your class already

believing that they are stupid, dumb, good for nothing...you fill in the blank. These children have already begun to buy into a belief system. People in their lives—parents, other family members or other teachers—have programmed these children into believing that they are something they are not. You and I both know that if you continually tell children they are stupid, they will believe it as their own truth by and by.

On the other side, we have all known students who enter our classrooms liking themselves, with tons of self-confidence, high self-esteem and a great foundation for living, learning and loving. These children, as we know, are no accidents either. Someone has assisted these children to form positive belief systems about themselves.

Belief systems come from three places:

1. *What we see*—what we have witnessed and know to be true because we saw it with our own eyes.

2. *What we experience*—what we know to be true because we lived through it.

3. *What we are told*—what we choose to believe because someone tells us it is so and we believe it.

We then decide how we feel about what we have seen, been through or been told. Belief systems are very fragile things, and all that is in them may not be correct.

Prejudice is an example of belief system programming. Prejudice is the belief system of one individual handed to another and believed, with or without evidence. I am not referring just to racial or ethnic prejudice; I am speaking about every kind of prejudice. I have watched it in families where the mother wants to have the children on her side, so she teaches her children prejudice about their father or stepfather.

So many times we buy into belief systems without hesitation, not stopping to investigate or gather our own data. It might be well for each of us to check out our belief systems and find out what is in them. What was valid for us when we were ten, fifteen or twenty years old may not be valid for us now.

When we operate from an obsolete belief system, we can become stagnant and bigoted. Outdated belief systems can cause us to be closed to new ideas. We can become defensive and rigid in our thinking and behavior. When we do, our students may follow our example.

How do we begin to rewire our belief systems? We begin by examining what we think. So often we operate from the "reaction-faction." We end up doing what we do because we always have, thinking what we think because we always have. Maybe it is time to look and see if there may be another way.

As educators, we can assist our students to challenge their belief systems and to learn that they will continually change, based on the information they have and what they learn as they live and grow. We can assist these youngsters to test their beliefs, not to take everything at face value.

Human beings who are willing to learn, grow and move forward assist us all to move forward. We can give our students permission to explore their thought processes and understand how they work, so the students can become self-reliant and self-confident and learn to elevate their own self-esteem.

Who Said That?

You are lying in bed on a Saturday morning; it is quite early, and you are just waking up. There is nothing in particular on your schedule and no particular reason to be in a hurry to get up. Yet there is this gnawing in your stomach that says you should get up. Who said that? Who is talking?

You are beginning a new project at school, and you are really excited about it. There is some challenge and some risk involved, although no danger. When it is successfully completed, there could be much personal recognition for you and your school in your district and possibly statewide. As excited and maybe a little frightened as you feel, there is this gnawing in your stomach that tells you that you can't do it. Who said that? Who is talking?

You are shopping and come across a real bargain on an antique that you have wanted for several years. The price is not to be believed. You take out your checkbook ready to purchase and be on your way to place your new treasure in its new place. Yet there is this gnawing in your stomach that tells you that you shouldn't spend the money. Who said that? Who is talking?

Meet the committee! The committee is made up of many people. You may find your mom and dad on the committee, a brother or sister, a teacher. It just depends on how you were raised. Begin to ask yourself, Who said that? Am I making this decision for myself, or is my committee attempting to get into the act? You may want to begin to explore the messages you received as a child and from whom they came.

We often find that we have strong messages from people

who played major roles in our lives. Many of the messages you were given as a child may have been very supportive of who and what you are today. I'm asking you to look at the messages that may not support you to be all you can be, achieve all you can achieve and really go for it in life.

One day as I got ready to leave after visiting my parents, I mentioned that I was going home to clean out my garage. My mother, who likes to tease, offhandedly said, "No, you won't." I felt as though I had been slapped across the face. I didn't say anything to her, but on the way home I thought about why I had reacted so quickly and felt so bad.

For the first time in my life, I realized that one of my mom's messages to me was, No you won't. I had incorporated that message into my belief system. Even though Mom was teasing because like everyone else I get sidetracked, I had taken her comment very seriously and bought the message. That day gave me a chance to explore my feelings and to begin to rewire my thinking. Now when I hear that message in my brain, I can do something about it instead of buying in.

If you have a committee in your head that causes you to constantly question your actions, you need to rewire your belief system. You need to get very clear about who you are today and what you are truly capable of being, doing and having.

As you become clearer on that information, it will be much easier for you to teach your students to do the same. You can then begin to teach from referent leadership, by example. Your students will take their lead from you, just as they do from their parents.

Listening to Your Gutometer

Your gutometer is located just above your belly and just under your sternum or breast-bone. Take the word gut and rhyme it with thermometer, and you have gutometer. It is the mechanism that lets you know when you are off track or something is not OK. Some of us are really good at listening to our gutometers, and some of us may not even be aware that we have one.

Your gutometer lets you know when you do not like someone, when you may be in some danger, when someone just told you a lie. It warns you with a silent alarm when things are not OK.

It also lets you know when you *are* OK. Sometimes your intellect may be going crazy, but when you check in with the old gutometer it lets you know that it's just your intellect being a little crazy and that everything is just fine.

When we are children our gutometers work really well. We listen to them and are tuned in most of the time. As we grow up, we stop listening to what we know and start paying more attention to what our established belief systems tell us.

Our gutometer is often aware of:

• which students need extra attention before challenging an assignment

• which parents need a reassuring phone call before report cards go home

• when an extra recess would avert behavior problems

• when to check in with the new teacher for a "you're doing great" chat

When you get really good at listening to your gutometer,

you can learn to check in when you are in doubt as to what to do about a certain situation. When you are speaking to someone and you are not quite sure what is happening, you can check in and see what the reading is on your gutometer.

I don't know about you, but when I follow my gut I rarely go wrong. It is when I ignore all the screeching of my trusty gutometer that I find myself in trouble. Along with learning to tell ourselves the truth about what we really think, we need to practice listening to what the rest of our systems are telling us, including sight (observation), hearing (listening) and experience from past situations.

The Words Without the Music

Have you ever been speaking with someone who seemed to be telling it like it is, and yet somehow you just didn't get it? The words were all there, the information seemed valid, the person seemed credible, yet something did not ring true. I call this the words without the music. When we talk about communication, there are a few standards that have to be met for me.

• The person communicating must be willing to look me in the eye when we speak.

• The speaker must be willing to ensure that I can repeat, with understanding, whatever he or she is attempting to say to me.

• I always retain the right to my own point of view.

• All systems need to be go for me; I need to hear the words and the music on all levels.

Students are very finely tuned to whether our words fit the music. A friend described a classroom where three seriously emotionally disturbed students would watch and listen carefully to "the music" each morning. If the teacher was not 100 percent present and speaking from a place of sincerity, one student would begin making sound effects, another would draw on anything handy and the third would interrupt constantly with TV vignettes. If the teacher was 100 percent with them and clear about what was happening, the students could stay with him for ten to fifteen minutes.

Ding and Clunk Communication

A "ding" communication goes right in and feels absolutely right on all levels. It is as though a bell has been rung and it is crystal clear and solid. A "clunk" communication goes in and lands in my belly like a rock, feels very uncomfortable and doesn't set right.

LIKE PARENT, LIKE CHILD

A parent approached a teacher about having her son stay in another classroom as a full-time student rather than being moved to another class three periods a day for special education. The teacher explained that he did not think the child was ready to give up the additional assistance he received in the special ed. class. The parent persisted; the communication hit the teacher with a "clunking thud."

Upon further investigation, the teacher found that the parent had an underlying need to be in control. The parent had gone to the school district, without the teacher's knowledge, and told the district office the teacher had authorized the change.

This teacher experienced a real "ding" when the school psychologist suggested that the child's control issues in the classroom were a direct reflection of the mother's style.

I am often asked what I do with clunk communication. Sometimes I just let it go, after making a note of it. If, however, this person and this information is important to me, I call upon the person delivering the information to clarify. Usually one of two things will happen: Either the person will repeat the communication, and I will get a ding; or we must have further conversation to clarify the point.

Unfortunately, I sometimes find that the person was not being totally honest with me. As uncomfortable as calling someone on this may be, I usually find that when I have been willing to ask for clarification and get down to the bottom of it, the next communication goes more smoothly.

When I allow clunk communication to go by me without handling it, it begins to erode my relationship with the person. I can become increasingly uncomfortable with him or her until I handle it.

Begin to pay attention to the kinds of communication you deliver and receive. Begin to notice if you can tell the difference in the delivery and reception of ding and clunk communication. See if you don't agree that the people you really trust and know you can count on communicate with ding communication. Your relationships with these people are cleaner and more comfortable than with those whose communication may not be as clear or honest.

Children are so perceptive that they pick up on ding and clunk communication immediately. One of the ways to assist students to elevate their self-esteem is to be aware of the times when student-teacher communication is not two-way, times when the teacher takes a position of being right simply because he or she is the teacher. Often in these types of interactions, the teacher's need to be right automatically puts the student in the wrong position. It rarely feels good to be placed in the automatic wrong position. Aware teachers try to stay congruent in communications, so that their students get more dings than clunks.

Being human enough to admit that you have been in error or to back down from a point when a student has proven his or her point gets high marks with me. As long as the interchange is founded in honesty and the facts are the facts, it is wonderful for a teacher to acknowledge the validity of a student's point. It can be a great win-win situation—a ding for all concerned!

Walking the Talk

Hand in hand with my integrity goes living what I say. It is really important to me that I am who I am in my living room, my office, on the platform or in front of a classroom. When

I am not "walking the talk," being who I am and living by the rules that I have for myself, the nonverbal message to others is that I am not who I say I am. The person I know I am is not aligned with the person I am willing to show to others.

Your students are looking to you at every moment to see who you are and what you are about at all levels. Whether we like it or not, they often want to grow up to be just like their teachers and parents.

When we are not passionate about what we teach or what we are doing, the message goes out that whatever we are dealing with is just so-so. Our students may very well decide that this is true.

Part of our ability to walk the talk and talk our walk is to believe in ourselves and who we are, so that when we are out there in the world what we say and what we do are in alignment with who we are. That is integrity.

If children learn very early to tell the truth at as many levels as possible and to be as honest as they can be, they grow up with a much healthier sense of self. When we learn the benefits of the truth, we usually don't have to use manipulative behavior to get what we want. Telling the truth allows us to ask for what we want in an honest way.

In order for children to be honest, they must feel safe asking for what they want. This is certainly true for adults as well. If telling the truth backfires on us, we learn other ways to get what we want. But our self-esteem suffers if we cannot get our needs met in open and honest ways.

It is possible to create a safe environment in your classroom where children can be honest. Even if children in your class do not have that kind of safety at home, they can learn it from you and carry it out into their lives. Unfortunately, in our world not all environments support this.

Does your classroom currently support your students to walk their talk, defining and telling the truth? When it does, the children entrusted to you can begin to learn not just the curriculum content, but also the process of how to have their lives work. That cannot happen unless you are paying attention to how your own life works and whether *you* are walking your talk.

Living What You Love, Loving What You Live

A big part of integrity is doing with my life what I love. Human beings are not living their full potential if they are doing something they hate.

When I am living what I am loving and loving what I am living, my life works much better. When I venture into the things I really do not have a passion for or allow myself, for example, to accept a speaking engagement on a subject that is not in my immediate area of interest, I notice that I am not as good as I am when I am speaking on and about something I love.

Are you as a teacher living what you are loving and loving what you are living? Are you making the difference you wanted to when you were a student and dreamt of what you would do with and for your students when it was your turn to teach? Do you go home at night feeling as though you have made a difference, or did you just put in another day? Do you trudge home to bed, get up tomorrow and do it all over again?

I cannot believe that we are intended to drag ourselves through life. I do not believe that we should do our life's work in a way that does not allow us to reach our full potential, and I believe that doing so is available to each of us.

Two things make it possible. First, knowing what it is you want, and second, being willing to do whatever it takes to have what you want.

Every year I speak to thousands of people about the quality of their lives and whether they are getting what they want. Teachers have a very special place in this world. Unlike word processors, fire fighters or executives, teachers have the minds and hearts of young people in their hands every day.

If you are hating what you do when you teach, your students are going to know it. They pick up on your resentment, anger and hostility. Unfortunately, whether or not it is directed at them, there is a good chance they will interpret your attitude and behavior as a direct reflection of how you feel about them.

They may decide, as many children do when parents argue, that they are responsible for your state of mind. Our attitudes, stress, anger and unhappiness get all over everyone around us. It is simply not fair for children to have one more opportunity to decide, based on someone else's attitudes, that they are not OK. I am quite sure you do not want that either.

I've challenged you from page one to examine who you are, what your personal integrity is and how it works in your life, to tell yourself and others the truth. Now I am suggesting that you look at the quality of your life and whether you are loving the experience of it.

If you are not loving the experience of your life, is that enough for you? Is that how you want the rest of your life to be? Most importantly, do you know you have a choice about that? Loving what you do serves your students in ways much beyond your specific curriculum objectives.

What You Think of Me Is None of My Business

This is the title of one of my favorite books. What Terry Cole-Whittaker says in this book is that each of us must find ourselves—all the things we have been talking about here—but when we do so, others in our lives may not be impressed.

People in our lives are used to us being the way we have always been. When we begin to make other choices, people in our lives may feel scared and insecure. We should be sensitive and patient with them. However, each of us deserves to make our choices from our own definition of integrity. Only through these choices will we achieve true freedom and peace of mind.

Now, I know what some of you are thinking: She has got to be kidding. She doesn't understand what my life is like, the pressures I am under, the job I have. She doesn't know my husband or wife.

You're right, I don't. But I know someone just like you or someone in similar circumstances. Your life and your career as a teacher could look very different a year from now—without leaving your school or even your classroom, without changing your contract or your residence.

Your experience of life can be what you want it to be 90 percent of the time. Are you willing to have it work that well? Are you also willing to care more about your own integrity than about what others think your integrity should be?

Are you willing to choose how you will behave regardless of how others think you should behave? Are you willing to take responsibility for the choices you make as an educator for the benefit of your students?

I am not for a moment suggesting that we be anything but loving, sensitive and wonderful with people. But I am suggesting that we each get aligned behind the truth for us. What makes your heart sing? Teach from that place of joy, and your students will learn not only content, but also honesty and integrity from a teacher who models these qualities at the highest levels.

If It's to Be,
It's Up to Me

Every human being has a few inherent desires; most of us have some of the same ones. One of these desires is to make a difference. We want to leave this planet knowing that we have touched people in a positive way.

It might be well for each of us to begin to examine why we have chosen the work of education. What is the contribution we are here to make? Is it still part of our life experience?

Why did you become a teacher? Was there a teacher in your life who inspired you to choose this profession? Was teaching something your parents thought might be a good career for you? Was it the path of least resistance? Why are you a teacher?

My concern for teachers is that the expectations we had when we entered the field of education may not be being fulfilled. Many teachers I know are disillusioned, frustrated and weary. They feel as though their hands are tied. They feel they cannot make the difference they intended to make. Circumstances generated either by themselves, their school situations or their environments are getting in the way.

We seem to be facing some of the most challenging times we have ever had in dealing with today's youth. These challenges, ranging from drugs to dysfunctional families, are stretching the resources of individuals, families and the educational system.

Yet, if we are to remain in the teaching profession (and some of us will to the sweet or bitter end), we must find a way to create a positive experience for ourselves as well as our students. Left alone, the system will continue as it is.

There is a law that says "to create the same result, continue to do what you are doing." If education is to change, it will be because teachers and parents are willing to do what needs to be done. It will change because teachers and parents are willing to go beyond what has worked in the past and look at new options and ideas.

Something Is Wrong with This Picture

Why are some schools exciting places to be? What creates the feeling that every classroom is alive? What encourages a collegial feeling among staff? What stimulates parents to participate in the process of their children's education?

Why do some schools feel like special, almost magical, places for children, while others lack soul? Why, in some schools, do teachers avoid the eyes of other teachers, avoid talking to each other and their students? What happens in a school where teachers snap at each other and at their students and lock up their classrooms the instant the last bell rings? Something is wrong with the picture.

Is it a question of money? Is it just an attitude? Or is it much more? Is it a loss of enthusiasm for the profession of teaching and educating? Looking at the field of education, we can see fabulous results in schools situated in impoverished areas. There are also horrendous results in schools where there is plenty of cash.

Pardon my jargon, but I believe the difference is the "come from" of the people involved. It appears to be a commitment not to settle for the ordinary or the way it has always been.

At McAuliffe School in Cupertino, California, it is a matter of teamwork. Everyone, parents and teachers alike, is committed to the highest quality education available. Everyone is involved, everyone assists with everything, and everyone is heard. Everyone benefits, but especially the children they have come together to serve.

Everything we do affects everything we do. Every action or nonaction we take affects us and those around us. We are like dominoes. When we move, we cause others to move. If you are cheerful and happy, those around you will react in a like manner; if you are crabby with your students, you will have a bunch of crabby students by lunchtime. If you take a stand to have your school be what you want it to be, at least in your classroom, you will affect those around you.

Enthusiasm is contagious—so is depression. Many times we are communicating most loudly when we say nothing. Eighty-seven percent of our communication is nonverbal. Pay attention to what you are communicating to your students, parents and fellow teachers about your classroom and your school.

What is the picture at your school? Who is responsible for the soul and the magic? Who is responsible for your personal happiness or dissatisfaction with the profession? The only person who can be held responsible for your feelings, be they joy or despair, is yourself. If something is wrong with the picture at your school, look first at yourself.

Where Are You in the Picture?

The first thing to look at is where you are. Is teaching what you want to do? Why? If the answer is yes, teaching is what you want to do, and you can define why, then the next question is, is it providing you with the experience of life you want?

If you are going to devote your adult working life to something, you should be enjoying the process. You may spend forty or fifty years as a teacher; you may already have been in the field a number of years. A little self-assessment is in order.

Those of us who are in service professions, and I consider teaching a service profession, sometimes decide that we are there to serve, period. Yet, to serve others from a place of true service, we must be taking good care of ourselves. If we are not taking good care of ourselves, we risk serving from a lesser level, serving from obligation rather than love. I have never met anyone who wants to be given to or taught from a place of obligation, have you?

The question is not, Is it without effort? Is it without challenge? Is it easy? The question is, Does teaching give you what you want? Do you enjoy it? Do you look forward to the challenge?

Are you thrilled when your students succeed? Do you see the successes, even the little ones? Do you still get excited in August in anticipation of a new school year? Do you love to set up your classroom for the new year? Do you enjoy planning a classroom celebration?

Do you like your students? Do you learn from your professional colleagues? Do you feel a sense of satisfaction that you have touched the lives of your students in a very special way? Would you choose again to be a teacher?

Students Know

Your students always know if something is not right with their teacher. We become so accustomed to our environments and the people around us that we sometimes stop paying attention to how much we know without anyone saying anything.

Walk into the teachers' lounge and just pay attention. See how much you can ascertain about what is going on without being told. If you have children of your own, I'd be willing to bet that they know what your mood is as you come in the door at night.

Our students pick up the same kinds of messages. They will know whether to run to you or from you. They will be afraid or unafraid to approach you based in part on your attitude and stance.

Some teachers appear to avoid interacting with students. I think these teachers and their students both pay a heavy price. Could it be that at some level these teachers feel as though all they have to offer their students is the content of their lesson plans? Or is something else going on here? Do these teachers feel inadequate to deal with the pressing and difficult issues their students may have?

A SPECIAL CLASSROOM

I recently visited a classroom for behaviorally disordered and incorrigible children. The teacher in this classroom had come to a point in her career when she had to choose between giving up her career in education or choosing to have it be different. In her twenty-year career, she had experienced many kinds of educational process, in many parts of the United States and Canada, including serving as principal of a remote Indian school.

She had seen many things work and many more not work. She was convinced that there had to be a better way to serve children. Her field of expertise was disturbed and behaviorally disordered children, so this was no small order.

She was becoming one of the disillusioned,

frustrated and weary teachers dragging across the parking lot early in the morning without a smile or spring in her step. Her health and general well-being began to reflect her passive attitude.

After attending several of my programs, she asked if she could adapt and use some of my concepts with her kids. My response was "go for it," and she did.

Although she was teaching in an economically depressed, rough neighborhood, her classroom was one of the most delightful classrooms I have ever had the opportunity to visit. Everywhere I looked, there was something to see, something to draw my attention to something else.

She hadn't spent a lot of money. Pictures were cut out of magazines with care to suggest dreams of things to come. Pictures of her students having fun with a loving teacher were posted. The room was filled with simple things made with great pride, inspired by a woman whose choice was to have it work, in one of the most difficult arenas and areas of town.

What I saw in that classroom was an ordinary young woman with a desire to have it be different in spite of the fact that the district, the budget, fellow teachers and a deteriorating school building all demonstrated that things would never change. As a result of this determination, these incorrigible children, one step from incarceration, remained on a regular school campus, and some were able to return to regular classrooms.

Self-Esteem

One of the most pressing issues for children today is low self-esteem, according to Robert W. Reasoner, a founding member and former president of the National Council for Self-Esteem who served 11 years as superintendent of the Moreland School District in San Jose, California. In Chapter 1 of his book *Building Self-Esteem,* Reasoner outlines five key points that assist human beings in building self-esteem.

BUILDING SELF-ESTEEM

Desired Outcome in Children	Adult Roles
1. A sense of security	• Set realistic limits. • Enforce rules consistently. • Develop self-respect and responsibility. • Build trust.
2. A sense of identity and self-concept	• Recognize children's strengths. • Demonstrate love and acceptance. • Aid students in assessing personal strengths and shortcomings.

Desired Outcome in Children	Adult Roles
3. A sense of belonging	• Create a proper environment. • Explore the responsibilities of group membership. • Encourage acceptance and inclusion of others.
4. A sense of purpose	• Convey expectations. • Build confidence and faith. • Aid students in setting goals.
5. A sense of personal competence	• Aid students in making choices and decisions. • Provide encouragement and support.

Reasoner also suggests that one of the primary ways to start building children's self-esteem is to build the self-esteem of their teachers. He notes that there are five issues to be addressed on the subject of low self-esteem among teachers.

1. *Teachers are expected to meet multiple expectations.* Expectations are so varied among parents, students and staff that teachers have a difficult time trying to determine priorities, then trying to evaluate their results.

2. *Teachers seldom define specific personal goals or expectations.* Reasoner contends that individuals who constantly have goals set for them find themselves doing things that might not be important to them. He notes that it is

difficult to establish one's own self-esteem based on the goals of someone else.

3. *Teachers rarely receive the kind of accurate feedback necessary for self-evaluation.* Teachers' feedback often comes by chance from other teachers, parents and staff. Lack of feedback leaves teachers without adequate information to evaluate their performance.

4. *The environment in many schools is not conducive to a feeling of self-worth.* General attitudes of caring, trusting and accepting individual methods and points of view are lacking in many schools. Mutual support among teachers and other staff often seems missing.

5. *Teachers seldom face their personal limitations realistically.* Most teachers want to do the very best job possible. They may go from idea to idea, trying to do it all, without recognizing their limits. When they let themselves down in their own eyes, their self-esteem plummets like a rock.

Ask yourself, Does this information pertain to me? Do I fit into these categories? How is my self-esteem?

As educators, we cannot teach and assist others to be winners if we see ourselves as losers. When I believe I am a winner I can be an example of what I teach. If I do not see myself as a winner, it is impossible to empower others to be winners.

What is a winner? Winners are people who understand who they are and how they operate in life. Winners give all of themselves to what they are doing. They love to have fun. They look for opportunities to improve things. They're not afraid to share their time, energy and knowledge. They understand their shortcomings as well as the shortcomings of others; they make allowances but no excuses.

We all have the potential to be winners. It takes only willingness and openness to learn another way or expand on what we are doing. Sometimes it simply means taking the time to acknowledge what we are already doing.

Choose to see yourself and others as winners. Look for things to acknowledge yourself for, rather than stuff to make yourself feel wrong about. No one outside yourself can make you happy. You have to do it for yourself, because you are the only one who has that kind of power over you. And your students need to learn that, too. It is one of the keys that will assist them to be able to create anything they want in their lives.

If You Can't Trust Yourself, Who Can Your Students Trust?

Trust is a cornerstone of self-esteem, just as integrity is the foundation. If I can't trust myself to take care of myself, I can't feel a high level of self-esteem. Without trust, I cannot believe in myself or in anyone else. My experience of life will be based in fear. I will fear that life will not support me, and I will not support myself.

If you are having a problem trusting yourself, if your self-confidence and self-esteem are shaky, what do you suppose your students pick up from you?

Think about how you feel about those around you who do not have high self-esteem or those who are not self-confident. How much credence do you give to what they say?

If someone wants me to do something, I am much more likely to do so when I pick up on his or her enthusiasm and excitement than if he or she is sluggish and wishy-washy about the request.

It is difficult to get students excited about self-esteem or social studies if you are not excited. It is impossible for human beings to trust people who do not trust themselves. In many cases, you will spend more waking hours with your students than their parents will. Your students must be able to trust who and what you are and what you stand for, for their sake and for your own.

It is much easier to learn from someone who trusts her- or himself than from someone who does not. People who have low self-esteem and low self-confidence are hesitant, timid, afraid to speak their minds or to offer a point of view. Or they may take a totally different tack and be very brusque, abrasive, offensive and aggressive, in an attempt to keep people from finding out just how scared they really are.

Rebuilding Credibility with Yourself

Rebuilding credibility with yourself is vital to stepping into or realigning integrity, and it's easier than you might think. If you are really interested in doing that, I have four easy suggestions, which you can begin now.

1. *Do not make agreements that you know in your heart of hearts you do not want to keep in the first place.*

2. *Commit to one thing to do for yourself and do it.* If it is exercise, then commit to that and do it daily. Throw away

the laundry list of things you are going to do, things that in reality, you know you will never get to. Commit to one action and do it.

3. *Do something nice for yourself every day.*

4. *Tell yourself the truth about what you are doing in your life and why.*

When you begin doing what you say you will do, when and how you say you will do it, you will begin to believe in you. Then you will know that others can believe in you, too.

I have taken a poll for years when I do my lecture on stress. The average adult will say that he or she keeps from 85 to 99 percent of all commitments made to others. Most adults are proud of that statistic. When teenagers are asked how many of their commitments to others they keep, they generally respond with 50 to 60 percent.

When the same group of adults is asked what percentage of commitments they keep to themselves, most responses are about half of the commitments they keep to others. Based on these numbers, would you say we value others more then we do ourselves?

If you inventoried your life, would you have more have-to's and shoulds or want-to's and choose-to's? Silly question, huh? Most of us would have more have-to's and shoulds. Our society functions with obligations to each other. The problem is that obligation creates anger, resentment and even physical illness.

Take a few moments to think about your current have-to's and shoulds and your want-to's and choose-to's. You may want to write them down. Then go back through the lists and think of a one-word description for how you feel about each item.

When we make choices that indicate that we think poorly of ourselves, it is difficult for others to think of us in any other terms. If we are not doing the things that take care of us, if we are not nice to ourselves, if we abuse ourselves and our bodies, it is pretty difficult for others to respect us. Others might like us, or even love us, if we are close friends or family members, but they won't grant us a high level of respect, admire how we live, aspire to be like us, or listen to our point of view.

If we want to be taken seriously, then we must take ourselves seriously. If we want to be held in respect, then we must respect ourselves. If we want to teach our students to have self-respect and integrity, then we must be living it, not just talking about it.

Each Journey Begins with a Step

Many people voice concerns about education. Certainly, any problems in education reflect larger problems in our cities, in our country, in our world. But these problems can't be solved until we as individuals take responsibility for making our personal lives work.

When we are willing to examine where we are in life, how we feel about it and what we want, we can begin making changes. Small changes by individuals can add up to larger changes in schools, districts, communities and society.

Is your life exactly the way you want it? Are your

students getting 100 percent from you each day? Do their parents cooperate with you in the task of educating their children? Do you want to create a different relationship with the children and teachers you work with daily? Do you want to make a bigger impact on education? Start small with the things you can change in yourself and your classroom—the positive ripple effects could be far-reaching.

You and Me
and Them

Here is some good news and some not so good news. Relationship is all there is. That's right, relationship is all there is. A relationship is any interaction people have with the other individuals that walk this planet. No man or woman is an island, and we all must deal with people all day long. Our ability to create workable relationships will determine our experience of life.

When was the last time you took your car in for repair, took your cat to the vet or had your washing machine repaired? When was the last time you asked another teacher for help on a project, requested approval from your principal for an exception to a rule or needed a parent to come to the classroom and assist for a morning? Their eagerness to help and their attitude about your request probably depended on the health of your relationship with them.

We are talking about every kind of relationship—family, friends, peers, casual acquaintances. You have a relationship with every human being you meet. You have a relationship with every student you teach. You have a relationship with yourself. You have a relationship with everyone and everything. How are your relationships?

Levels of Relationship

Chances are, you and I do not want to be best friends with everyone we meet. We haven't time. The world is not set up so that we will find every human being aligned with who we are and what we want. I find that there are several levels of relationship.

Committed. Picture a small circle. You are the circle. Immediately around your circle are two or three other circles. These circles represent your 'til-death-do-us-part relationships—your spouse, your parents, your children and, perhaps, one or two very close friends.

Close Friends. Around this group is another set of circles. These represent what I call your good-news-bad-news-I'm-here friends. These are people you are pretty close to, people you can depend on to some degree. These are people you play with, share life with, call upon when things are really up or really down.

Occasional Friends. Around this group there is another set of circles. These represent what I call your day-to-day supporters. These are usually people you work with, fellow teachers, neighbors, maybe a few of your students' parents, friends you make plans to see now and then.

Casual Acquaintances. Another set of circles, and these are what I refer to as bread-and-butter-conversation people. Even though you may see these people every day, you simply exchange pleasantries. How are you? I'm fine, and you? You may pass them each day without any meaningful interchange.

Brief Encounters. Again another set of circles. In most cases, the majority of the people in your life are here. You rarely know their names; you might not even recognize their faces. You may not ever talk to them. A clerk at a department store or a waitress or flight attendant are in this category.

Now where do our students, their parents, our fellow teachers and the administrators we work with fit? Let's begin with our students. Our students need to feel, in the time that they spend with us, that they move very quickly into the *committed* circle or at least the *close friends* circle.

Children need to feel that we will do whatever it takes to have them win. It is our responsibility to have the relationship with our students work. We have the tools or, at least, access to them. That is why we are called teachers.

I believe parents can fall into any of the categories of relationships. Some will feel like very close friends by the end of the year, while others you may not have even met by the end of the year.

Some teachers have expressed a fear that allowing students to get too close to them might not serve the students, but I disagree. To learn to be close to someone and then to say good-bye is a healthy lesson. It is part of life's process.

Students can benefit from understanding the process of relationships and how they work. We are taught many kinds of things in the educational process of 12 years, but how relationships work, what the levels of relationship are and how we move from one to another may not be among them.

As I looked at the circles of my relationships, I began to ask myself, beyond my family, how did these people get into my circles? Did they just show up, or did I invite them? Did they earn their way there, or did I appoint them?

I began noticing similarities and differences. Some of these people I wanted there; some of them I did not. If I did not want them, why were they there? Did I add to the quality of their lives? Did they add to the quality of mine?

The list of questions goes on and on. What was my level of trust with these people? How did they move from one circle to another? How did they move closer and farther away from me? Did I make that decision, or did they?

More important to me than the placement within a specific circle was the quality of my relationships with these people. What was I giving? What was I getting? How honest could I be with them, and they with me? Did I really show up for them, or just put up with them? If something was really bothering me, did I have people in my life who would be there if I called, no matter what time it was?

There is real value in deciding where people fit in your life, who you want to be there and who you would prefer be elsewhere.

Every Relationship Is an Assignment

I believe that everyone in your life and mine is there for a reason; each person is there to teach and there to learn. Every time we have an exchange with someone, negative or positive, we have an opportunity to learn something or to teach something. Even the people in your *brief encounters* circle can provide valuable lessons in life.

A Freeway Encounter

Several months ago I was going to Pasadena on business. My plane landed about 7:30 a.m. I picked up my rental car and drove onto the 210 freeway toward Pasadena.

At that commute hour, traffic was heavy, and everyone was going quite fast. As I headed onto a section that would take me up and over the lower deck, I saw an incredible thing. A white Mazda RX7 that was in the slow lane spun out. It did four large spins from right to left across the freeway. I stared in disbelief as cars swerved this way and that to avoid this whirling white dervish. By some miracle, all the traffic missed the car. It came to rest on the opposite side of the freeway, in the fast lane, facing the wrong way. No one stopped; everyone continued as though nothing had happened.

I pulled off the freeway, got out of my car, walked to the Mazda, opened the door and pulled out a sobbing, semi-hysterical woman who kept saying, "Did you see what they did? They ran me off the road." I put my arms around the woman, who collapsed into them and sobbed as though her heart would break. She finally calmed down enough to explain that a blue Bronco had forced her off the road, causing her car to spin out. There we stood— two women, total strangers, holding one another and comforting each other on a busy freeway.

Suddenly a third car, a blue Bronco, sped up and stopped. A third woman jumped out, also crying. She ran over to the woman in my arms, saying over and over again, "I am so sorry; I didn't see you; please forgive me." The first woman turned from me to the newcomer, and they melted into a sobbing embrace of please forgive me's and it's OKs.

When both women had calmed down, we figured out how to get the white Mazda RX7 turned around in the right direction. Once that was accomplished, the blue Bronco, then the white Mazda and then the little rental car pulled onto the freeway. There we were, three across, speeding down the freeway; the blue Bronco exited, the white Mazda exited. I was again driving down a freeway in Los Angeles, marveling at the lessons and gifts that three women who would never see one another again, who didn't even know each other's names, had taught each other in half an hour on a Tuesday morning.

One woman had injured another, if only by scaring her. Another, seeing the event, stopped to comfort the injured party. The first woman got a rare opportunity to say she was sorry for her action, while the second woman got to forgive. I felt luckiest of all; I got to observe the beautiful lessons these total strangers taught each other.

Every student, every parent, every brother, every sister who enters my room comes as both a teacher and a student. I am also both a student and a teacher. If we watch carefully, we all teach and learn.

Isolation Is a Choice

As I visit schools around the country, I notice that some faculty members are friendly and helpful; they will do just about anything to help out other staff, students or parents. Their energy seems bottomless. Their first response to any request is usually positive.

Yet on another campus in the same city, there seems to be an atmosphere of animosity and underlying anger and resentment. The children in these two environments seem to pick up on the teachers' attitudes. They reflect it right back in their own attitudes toward each other and their educators. Why, I've wondered, are two schools with the same economic structure, similar students from similar backgrounds, just a few miles apart, so dramatically different?

Upon further investigation, one thing becomes crystal clear. The faculty on one campus has learned how to communicate and form healthy supportive relationships with each other. Students seem to learn from this example and pick up their cues from their teachers.

The students at the second school also watch their teachers. These students are negative, uncooperative and generally unfriendly with students in neighboring classrooms, as they follow the example of their teachers. The faculty at the second school either does not know how to communicate in a way that works or simply chooses not to.

Whatever the reason, the teachers and students at the second school are paying a heavy price. Walking into that atmosphere each day takes a toll on the human spirit. Waking up each morning knowing that you must face negative attitudes cannot support people in the quest to have their lives work.

Not only that, but have you noticed that such an attitude gets all over everybody and everything? It gets on school secretaries, custodians and bus drivers. Everyone who comes in contact with that energy is affected by the negativity. It is hard, almost impossible, to promote self-esteem in this atmosphere.

Children, adolescents and adults often choose to isolate themselves from their world when it becomes too painful to continue in the fashion they have been attempting to live their lives. They choose isolation because it seems to be the path of least resistance, the least painful way to survive.

Sometimes it may seem like an effort to stop by another classroom for a visit or to invite a teacher you would like to get to know better to spend some off-campus time together. Maybe there is a subject or problem that could use a good brainstorming session—initiate it!

If adults do not model positive, working relationships for children, children cannot form relationships with peers, teachers or themselves. Sometimes our ability to form relationships depends on our feelings of worthiness, on our past experience of our world and on whether we perceive the world to be a friendly or a lonely place.

As educators, we must look at our own sense of worthiness and level of self-esteem. We cannot expect to assist in elevating the self-esteem of our students if by example, we have chosen isolation instead of working at relationships.

Sometimes the Best Choice Is Goodbye

I don't think we were meant to have close and intimate friendships or relationships with everyone. Sometimes it is best to evaluate our relationships to see if they are working for us and giving us what we need to have.

It all goes back to integrity. Am I telling myself the truth about a situation or a relationship? If we look at our levels of relationship, we can see that not everyone in our lives will be there forever. There is a lesson in that as well.

People and friends have a tendency to come and go in our lives. Someone we may be very close to may move or be transferred. We say goodbye and move on. Students, parents and assistants will come and go each year in a natural progression.

Some of us may have relationships that drain our energy. Perhaps we have made several attempts to confront what is not working and have found the other person unwilling to confront or to move to resolution about an issue that's important to us. Well, we are then back to choice.

Do I care enough about this person, are they important enough in my life, to accept this behavior? You are the only one who can answer for you. Some situations are so uncomfortable that they are not worth the pain and the price being paid. We can either move away from these relationships or take a stand.

What about the case of a student, parent or administrator? Here you are in a classroom situation with a person whom you might not choose to interact with out in the world. Yet, in this situation, you face the possibility of having her or him with you for an entire year.

As I see it, it is my responsibility to have everyone win. This person is in my environment. Whether I like the other person or not is not the issue. The invitation was issued when I claimed the classroom as my own. Inherent in that agreement was the agreement that I would be committed to my students and their parents for this school year. This agreement may mean assisting them to choose to go elsewhere if the situation doesn't work.

Before we get to that point, however, it is my responsibility to do everything I can to make it work. I have the advantage here; they are at a disadvantage. I am on my home turf. I know the rules, how the game is played and what my rights are. They do not. This is not their environment, they only visit here—they are guests.

Elizabeth Kuebler-Ross says, "Life tosses us into a

tumbler; it is up to us whether we are gnashed or polished." In this case, the tumbler is a sticky relationship. Every relationship is an assignment. I think we are in an excellent position here to have everyone learn.

The first step may be a simple conversation to ascertain what the issues are, and sometimes that is all it takes. Once in a while, I find a conversation with myself on the issues is what is needed, a conversation where I get real honest with myself about what I need to do to clean up the relationship.

Be willing to look beyond the apparent for a solution, just as you would with a family member. If there are no ways to have it work, then look for the best way to move the student or to have someone else deal with the parent. Most important is that you, the student and the parent all win. If anyone loses, we all lose.

And what about administrators? In some ways, they have what I call the power of the pen, and this can be intimidating to us. I do not think the rules of relationship change based on the players. Do whatever it takes to work problems out. Enlist the assistance of those who can help. If it gets to the point where the relationship becomes non-workable, stop and look at all of your options, and choose for the highest good of all concerned. The highest good could mean a move on your part. Remember, endings are also beginnings.

As painful as it might be, sometimes the best choice is goodbye. Staying in a relationship that does not add value and happiness to your experience of life is usually not the best choice for you. Such a relationship may look pretty good to the other person; yet, it may not support them either in the long run.

But what about family relationships, where you have a 'til-death-do-us-part commitment? My experience in twenty years of working with people has indicated that as we begin to clean up our own lives, others are forced to some degree to shift and change.

Whenever I have confronted a family member or anyone with love in my heart and the right intention, I always feel better. Although I might not get the other person to behave differently, I have expressed my point of view.

When I tell my truth to anyone, family member, friend or casual acquaintance, my perception of the situation often changes, even when the other person really doesn't do anything. Sometimes I find that people had no idea I was even upset. Fifty percent of the people you are angry with probably don't know it.

Support Doesn't Look Like Giving In

Do you know the difference between helping and assisting? When we help other people, we can cripple them; when we assist them, we can empower them. What does support in a relationship look like?

On the level of brief encounters, support may look like letting the other guy into the line, or maybe just giving a smile or a kind word. As we move up the levels of relationship, support and how it looks becomes more complicated.

In relationships that work, we support each other's

integrity. We don't let each other get away with behavior that does not support us in having our lives work.

A REASONABLE ATTITUDE

A teacher was being supported by the aides and other students in the class in requiring a reasonable attitude from an irate student before a further discussion on privileges could continue.

Reasonable attitude in this class was defined as making eye contact, having an open and relaxed body position, facing the person you were talking with and using a reasonable tone of voice. The teacher took the position that nothing else would happen until the matter of attitude was settled and that the agreed upon rules of the classroom would prevail.

The irate student refused to calm down and continued his loud, vocal protests about unfairness. He removed himself from the classroom and marched to the vice principal's office. The vice principal listened, then asked the student to wait while she went to the classroom in question. In the classroom, she asked the other students in the class how they saw the situation. The class, by consensus, wanted the rule for reasonable attitude to prevail. The students felt that the angry student was not living by the agreement, and they supported their teacher.

The vice principal returned to her office and

requested a reasonable attitude from the troubled student, who had now calmed down and complied. She did not discount the student's feelings, but supported the class and teacher in the groundrules that had been agreed to. She suggested that the student consider re-aligning with those groundrules.

The student was allowed to see that he could be supported in what he wanted to communicate, even if not agreed with, if he communicated in ways that worked rather than manipulating others with his anger.

The teacher in this class also has a list of support comments created by students. He has his students take one minute daily to acknowledge and support classmates for special achievement, outstanding citizenship or simply going out of their way to support or assist.

THE SAFETY PINS

Sometimes the need for support manifests in the student who constantly seeks help in the form of explanations, bathroom privileges, pencil sharpening, etc.

One very bright third-grade teacher coped with this type of situation with a student named Sally.

The teacher issued five safety pins to Sally each morning. Sally could turn these safety pins in any time she wished during the day in return for help or an explanation. When the safety pins were all in the hands of the teacher, the privilege of asking for help was used up until the next day, when Sally again was issued five safety pins.

The plan assisted Sally to learn to prioritize her requests and eliminated lots of unnecessary attention-getting devices. Sally began to be far more self-reliant, as well as to develop some new strategies for problem solving. She learned to get what she needed in ways that empowered her rather than in ways that continued to support her dependence.

When we observe children on the playground, we can quickly see profound examples of the importance of developing relationships. If children do not see examples of workable, healthy relationships, they will find it difficult to develop such relationships on their own. Sometimes you and your environment may be the only example these children have of what is possible in healthy relationships.

You probably spend more waking hours with your students than their parents do. Students will learn not only your lesson plan but your behavior.

6

Working Relationships
Take Work

For relationships to work, each of us must look to see who we are, how we feel about ourselves, how we feel about the world around us and how we feel about the other people in our world. We must also be able to tell ourselves the truth about situations and how we feel about them. Then we must learn to communicate our truth to others.

The most important relationship to examine is your relationship with yourself. To have healthy relationships with others, we must first have a healthy relationship with ourselves. We need to know how we feel about who we are, how we perceive ourselves and how we think the world perceives us.

Reaching In

Reaching in involves the willingness to look inside and see what is there. Reaching out involves the willingness to ask someone else what they see in the same situation, the willingness to look at something from another perspective.

If I see myself as a loser, a procrastinator, someone incapable of accomplishing things in my life, then I take that image into each interaction with other people. If I am angry with myself for things I should be doing or should have done, if I am afraid I will never accomplish them, then chances are excellent that I will reflect that anger back to the others in my life. What are you reflecting to your students?

Often, we look to see how other teachers are dealing with similar problems, how the principal thinks we should deal with a problem, how we think others will think we should deal with a problem, or perhaps how our parents might have dealt with a problem. We have a lot of trouble telling ourselves the truth about how we feel about different situations. As a consequence, we often make decisions based on our reaction to past situations or the actions or feelings of others.

I call this tendency the reaction-faction. We have a knee-jerk reaction, rather than stopping to look inside and telling ourselves the truth about how we feel right this minute about a situation. If we want to help young people be honest about their feelings, then we must first tell ourselves the truth about our own feelings. Then we and our students can live healthier and more productive lives. We model this behavior for children, and it can have a strong influence on how they feel about themselves.

TEARS AND TAPE

A little six-year-old girl came to class with tears on her face because she had torn her paper and expected to be in trouble. The teacher, buried in business, at first felt irritated that the child had not been more careful. But having heard my lecture on the reaction-faction, the teacher looked inside and decided that there wasn't, in truth, any anger there. He reached out for the tape and a tissue. He wiped away the tears, took the little girl on his lap and thanked the child for the opportunity to use the tape. He reminded the little one that without torn papers, there is not much use for tape.

Practice makes reacting from truth much more comfortable than reacting from what we may have been programmed to do or feel or what we think we *should* do or feel.

Reaching Out

Reaching out was an important step for me. It began when I wanted to find out why I did not have in my life what I wanted to have and why I did not have the relationships I wanted with others. I didn't understand the way people reacted to me. I found myself feeling defensive when I really did not know if it was warranted. I felt lonely and isolated. I couldn't understand why others could not see what a wonderful, warm and lovely person I was.

I began to explore my world and to look outside the

world I had been raised in. I took notice of other people who seemed to have a different point of view about life. Their cheerfulness got on my nerves. Didn't they know that life is about hard work and struggle? Didn't they realize that you had to be careful whom you became friends with, because people usually could be depended on to hurt you? It was a shock to me that everyone did not live day to day with conflict, chaos and crisis. That reality did not, however, teach me what I needed to know, only that there might be a different way to live.

Through years and years of programming, we may have been lead to believe that our feelings did not count. We may have gathered much evidence that we really did not have much to say or to contribute. If we believed the evidence, whether it was valid or not, we can now be at a place in life where we do not trust our own perceptions of the world, what we see or how we feel about it.

Very few of us grew up in the Brady Bunch. Most of our parents were out there striving to make a living and raise a family. Most of us grew up thinking that this is just how life is, each of us in our own little world. We never realized how very different these worlds might really be. Because our worlds were merged with only a few other worlds (families), our belief system told us that that is the way the world is everywhere.

What did the behavior of others and how they related to us teach us about who we are? Even more importantly, what do we now believe in turn and teach others about themselves?

Sometimes in this busy world we do not take time to look at how our lives are working, whether we are happy or how we feel. Maybe the first step for each of us is to realize that there may be a different, better way to have life work. We may need to do a little research.

In my reaching out process, I had to be willing to consider the possibility that as good (or bad) as my life was, maybe there was more—more that I could enjoy and more that I could give.

THE PARTY

Many of us grew up not trusting our own perceptions of the world. I remember a party my parents had when I was young. One of their guests was very intoxicated. I was too young to realize what was happening, but I knew something wasn't right. As a matter of fact, everyone was beginning to get a little strange. I was frightened when one man became really violent and obnoxious. I remember my dad telling me everything was fine and not to worry.

A little later, the man fell and was taken to the emergency room for stitches in his head. Now I was really worried. There was blood everywhere; at least, that's how it looked to me at age four. Yet the people I trusted most, my parents, kept telling me that everything was fine, not to worry, that there was no problem.

My parents were denying my perceptions. It happens to all of us in a million ways. I don't think it was or is intentional on the part of teachers and parents. I only know, after working with thousands of people, that our perception of life is often skewed. Many of us do not trust our own ability to see and determine clearly what we see and to decide how we honestly feel about it in the moment.

As a human being who has chosen education as your current life's work, how do you begin the process of reaching out into the world? The assumption is not that you are not involved, but that teaching can be very isolating. It generally places you on this tiny island with twenty to thirty children and maybe an aide, with some desks and easels floating nearby.

Reaching out may be as simple as visiting the classroom next door or the one down the hall. It may involve more than perfunctory hellos in the hallway.

Reaching out begins with reading books such as this one to expand the thought process. Reaching out may involve choosing to do some things that are personally stimulating to you—going to the opera or symphony, attending a play or even acting in one! It involves risking personally, exploring the world beyond your front door, your classroom and the schoolyard.

Reaching out may mean signing up for a workshop on human development. It may mean taking a good look at your behavior with others and your feelings today versus fifteen or twenty years ago. It may mean attending the next forum or conference on self-esteem.

Freshen up your life a bit. Reaching out can begin with a good heart-to-heart walk and talk with a good friend, in the park or by the shore.

Yes, I Am Not Listening

A writer once said, "Be more interested than interesting." I like that; I work on remembering that. Being genuinely interested and listening to others is an important part of workable relationships. You can make a tremendous difference in the lives of the people around you when you take the time to listen and show a genuine interest in how they are and what is going on for them.

Have you ever noticed how your students will behave to get your attention? Have you ever observed the face of a child who has begun to share something important when an adult turns his or her attention in another direction, ignoring the little one's attempt to communicate? Often, we don't even know we have done it.

Listening is one of the greatest gifts we can give our students and fellow teachers. I mean really listening; giving full attention to the other person, with eyes open and focused on the speaker, body relaxed, not involved in any other activity, actively acknowledging with nods and words that we do hear what is being said; listening without interrupting.

Listening can be very difficult. It requires concentration and patience. It requires putting your interests, your points of view and yourself aside. It requires giving your undivided attention to the other person. It may mean biting your tongue and refraining from offering judgment or solutions or telling your own story.

The results can be phenomenal. Listening lets other people know you really care about them, who they are and how they are.

I cannot overemphasize the importance of acknowledging and listening to your students. I am continually amazed at the difference I can create in my classes by simply making sure that I have in some way acknowledged each of my students before I begin teaching.

I make it a point to personally introduce myself and to be available to people. I really put forth my best effort to listen to what they say and remember the information for later use at lunch or a break.

Although most of my students are adults, they respond to that personal attention with attentiveness and are less likely to act out or act up. I believe it is because they feel acknowledged as individuals. They realize that I am personally invested in each of them, there to insure that they get what they have come for. As a result, they are more receptive to what I have to teach.

Getting Feedback

A very valuable tool for me on my journey through life has been the feedback of others, both verbal and nonverbal. Feedback lets me know how I am doing and if what I am doing will give me the result I want.

Feedback is one of the most valuable gifts my fellow life

travelers can give me. Of course, I have to be willing to listen to feedback. I often have to reach out and be willing to ask for it. It rarely helps me if I do not solicit it.

What exactly is feedback? In the broadest sense, it's to do just that— "feed back" what one has received. Webster's definition is "the transfer of part of the output back to the input, as of information."

Each of us has what I call a blind side—a side of us that is not apparent to us and that we cannot see. Sometimes this side of us can be causing us a great deal of trouble, and we won't even know it; we only know that something is not right.

I met a wonderful woman in one of my recent workshops. She is a kindergarten teacher in a co-op school in the San Francisco Bay area. She decided to participate in an ongoing personal growth program that involved several other women, some teachers and some from other walks of life. At times she was warm, sweet and just a joy to have in the group; at other times, she would become belligerent, defensive, dictatorial and difficult. Following these latter episodes, she would be very embarrassed and become very quiet.

After one particularly difficult evening, she asked to speak to me privately. She was very near tears. We went into a private office and sat down across from, but close to one another. (I do not believe in barriers in good conversation.) Firmly yet gently, looking her directly in the eye, I asked what was up.

It all came tumbling out. The same behavior that was getting her into a mess with the group was causing her problems at school. Fellow teachers shunned her; parents were rude and argumentative; she was having a real problem getting her ideas across at faculty meetings. Most important, she felt her marriage was in real jeopardy as a result of her attitude.

She was confused, because she felt justified in her actions and what she thought. She could not understand why other people did not see her good intentions, why they seemed so allergic to her, and why she reacted the way she did. Could I help?

It was very obvious to me what was happening here, yet, there was a risk involved in continuing this conversation. She was requesting feedback, and I certainly had a point of view to offer. The risk was whether she really wanted to hear what I had to say.

So I asked her if she wanted some feedback on the situation. I explained that feedback is simply my point of view and that she should take what she wanted and consider the rest my opinion. She said she would listen.

I had some pretty difficult things to offer, and she wept as she listened. I spoke from my heart and told the truth. I felt that control was the root of her problem. She felt that she was the only one that could do what needed to be done the way that it needed to be done. She allowed no space for other people's opinions or ways of doing things. Her attitude and behavior offended people and caused them to feel inadequate and of little value. But when others reacted, she intensified her actions, and it got her into trouble.

An amazing thing happened—she really listened to the feedback. She allowed herself to feel hurt and angry at first, and then she really took it to heart. In about six months, this woman's life experience was almost completely different. I have had lots of time to observe her in different arenas—at her school, in her home, with dozens of her friends, with her family, in the original group. She has totally flipped her attitude.

She has created miracles at her school. Her students, parents, fellow teachers and administrators are receptive, loving and appreciative of all she contributes and allows them to contribute.

She told me that if she had not been willing to ask for and receive the feedback she needed to find out what was not working, she would have left the school and her marriage. Instead, she is happier than she has ever been, and so is her family.

I've been asked if I thought students should have the right to give their teachers feedback. My answer is, Absolutely. If we are smart, we will set up our classroom environment in that fashion. We can teach our students to receive and deliver constructive feedback from and to each other, as well.

Doing so can create and cultivate an environment of honesty and trust. It can assist our students to learn that telling the truth and receiving the truth can assist us all to have stronger relationships with each other. Our students can also begin to see the value of listening to the points of view of others and learning to filter out what they feel may not serve them.

Risking to ask another human being what they see in us and then being willing to listen can have untold value.

Tips on Giving and Getting Feedback

Always create an agreement to deliver feedback. Don't just launch into telling someone about what they cannot see without asking if they want to hear it or are open to hearing it.

Always speak from your heart and not your intellect or anger.

Always tell the truth and work at keeping your agenda out of it.

Always talk about the behavior, not the person. The person is always perfect; the behavior is what needs to be worked on.

If possible, end with a hug and follow up later to see if your additional support is needed.

If you ask for feedback:

• Listen with an open heart.

• Allow yourself space to react to and digest what is being said.

• Ask for feedback from those you trust.

• Remember to thank them for their honesty.

• Use what you can and bless the rest.

Feedback delivered in anger is called something else. Filter the feedback you receive, because the person delivering it is always speaking through his or her own filters.

Confrontation Without Fear

As I look at the topic of relationships, I have often asked

myself what causes some to work so well and others to struggle. Relationships that once worked sometimes fall apart, ending in hurt and heartache. Still other relationships seem so difficult and then for some unknown reason settle down and turn into blessings.

Often in my workshops, I have people separate into small groups. In these small groups, I ask them to list the ten most important things in a relationship. Then I ask them to prioritize the items by consensus.

Without exception, no matter what the male and female mix or the number of people in the process, the thing the groups list as most important is communication. Communication, the one thing we most often find difficult, is also the one thing that we feel is most important.

When we then get down to what is important about communication, we get words like *honesty, truth, integrity.* Look at the following diagram and see if you can conclude what it is really about.

meet → confront → play → intimacy

The first thing that happens in any relationship is that we meet. Sometimes we meet several times in one day if we work or live with someone. A meeting means a coming together of two people. Now the next thing that must happen is that we confront. Confrontation for many of us is a scary word that produces immediate lumps in our stomach, but it need not do so.

Confronting need not be negative. Sometimes there may

be undelivered communication that needs to be dealt with. Sometimes there is just information to be imparted. Confronting means keeping current with the communication that needs to be shared with this individual.

I did not say grab people by the throat and choke them until they are unconscious on the concrete. Confront means to tell the truth. In its simplest form, confront means to look inside, to ask how things are.

Sometimes I walk to the front of a room and look out at the audience and there is someone there whom I immediately feel uncomfortable about. Of course, I am not going to walk up to this person and say, "Excuse me, but you bother me." But I know I have to get to the bottom of it for myself, or it will get in the way of my addressing the subject at hand.

So, I look inside and confront myself about my discomfort. I usually find that this person reminds me of someone or that this person is communicating resistance to me or the subject. Then I can move on. Chances are that I will never communicate with or confront the other person involved; it isn't necessary.

Play follows confrontation when we stay current with our communication. The atmosphere lightens up; tension lessens or disappears. We can then move on to intimacy. In most cases, intimacy does not refer to sexual intimacy, but to a deeper form of relationship.

THE LATE VOLUNTEER

A parent has agreed to be in your classroom each Thursday by 10:30 a.m. This is where you meet. Each and every Thursday, this parent arrives at 10:45. The late arrival throws your lesson plan off. You are beginning to feel irritated that this continues to happen.

At this point, you have a choice—confront it or let it continue. If you do not confront it, you can continue to let it bother you or choose to accept that this person is always going to be late.

The situation worsens. The parent gets a little later each week, and you feel a little more frustrated. Meanwhile, a price is being paid for your unwillingness to handle this.

Who is paying? You are paying in unnecessary stress. Your class is paying in having to put up with your attitude. Oh, you say, they don't know. Don't kid yourself. Kids know.

Finally, the parent is paying. He or she is watching you get more and more irritated without knowing why. She or he may have decided that you don't like her or him. This parent may have no clue as to why the situation has gotten so uncomfortable, especially if you are *saying* that everything is fine; in reality you are *communicating* something else.

Why don't we confront what is not working? We are afraid we will blow up the situation, and the other person will walk away. Depending on how important that person is to us and our level of investment in the relationship, we may not be willing to risk confronting and losing.

Well, I have some news. If we do not confront, the chances are that in the long run we will lose anyway. An uncomfortable situation will generally get worse if not confronted. A relationship in which communication is not open and problems are not handled will eventually end. Often, neither party is exactly sure what happened.

There are two possible ends to the late parent story. The situation can go unconfronted until the parent feels so uncomfortable she or he either just doesn't show up or says she or he can no longer volunteer. Or the parent will come in late another morning and at recess you will ask if it is a problem for him or her to be at school at 10:30 a.m.

Now, wouldn't it be interesting if you found out that this parent thought all along that he or she was supposed to be at school at 10:45? Or suppose the parent responded with some concrete reason that 10:30 would not work, but offered to stay an extra 15 minutes? What if the parent said he or she didn't think it mattered much to you, because you never seemed to notice his or her arrival or departure? Whatever the response, you can see that the chances of resolving the issue improve measurably when it's brought up and discussed.

Once we come together *(meet)* and discuss *(confront)* the situation with the parent and reach another agreement, the atmosphere in the classroom lightens measurably *(play)*. We then leave the situation with a new understanding of the individual and a stronger relationship *(intimacy)*.

In this case, we used an occasional friend as an example. We may never want this relationship to go beyond that level. In our more meaningful relationships, the relationship and its depth may well depend on our willingness to confront both the good and the bad.

Think about a relationship you once had that is no longer in the form it once was—a marriage, a work association, a friendship. Now ask yourself how much changed because of unwillingness to confront what did not work or hurt feelings or some misunderstanding. Fear and pride often cost us dearly when they keep us from communicating the truth and confronting what is there.

If we do not move from *meet* to *confront* to *play* and then to *intimacy*, the true level of intimacy available in relationships of every kind will never be reached. You cannot have that level of relationship if there is an unfinished agenda of hurt or anger underlying it.

I address this subject in the classroom as I would the feedback process. We learn about it and use the tools to create an open, honest and pleasant environment for learning.

Children are so perceptive. They know whether to run from us or to us. They are constantly testing to see how we feel about them and those around us. One of the most destructive situations that can develop in the classroom occurs when irritation with a child is not dealt with. The irritation can stem from muddy shoes, misbehavior in assembly, note passing or a constant need to sharpen pencils. We have a tendency to stew silently instead of dealing with the situation head on.

But we can create an agreement that works, with consequences if there is an infraction, and follow through. In this case, we would recognize the problem when it happens (meet), discuss it and come to an agreement (confront), acknowledge ourselves for handling it (play) and then offer a high five, a hug or whatever other method you and your students use to express celebration (intimacy) with one another. As we continue to do this with our students, we develop the kinds of relationships that offer them another example of what workable relationships look like.

What Works, Works

There are some universal rules in the world. They never change; they probably have always been there and probably always will be; they always work and they never fail. They work in this country, in every city, in your classroom, in your home, in every relationship, in every business without exception.

Do I have your attention? Here are the rules:

Keep agreements. If you make an agreement, keep it or renegotiate it to the satisfaction of the person with whom you have the agreement.

Tell the truth. Look inside and tell yourself the truth about the situation at hand. Then choose for the highest good of all concerned and move forward.

Respect life in all forms. Allow and leave space for all forms of life to exist and do nothing to harm others to the best of your ability.

Make sure others win. The best way to ensure that I get what I want is to make sure that others in my life get what they want. If we were all more concerned with everybody winning, then no one would have to lose.

Oh, you say, the world just does not operate that way. Yes, some of the world does operate that way. And furthermore, the part of the world that does works really, really well.

What part of the world is that? you might ask. The places where people are truly taking responsibility to have the world work and their lives work as well.

The Rules of Respect Do Not Change

Many adults think that because they are adults they have a right to be respected by children and young adults. Some adults also seem to think that respect is not necessarily a two-way street, that it is not important to treat youngsters or people perceived to be beneath them with respect.

To a great degree, respect is earned. Inherent in most interaction with others is a degree of respect. In much of society in this country, it is a common courtesy extended to one another like a handshake. Maybe there are degrees of respect just as there are degrees and levels of relationship. When I use the word *respect,* it speaks to some specific things.

Respect means holding other human beings with honor. Respect is the choice to ensure that the bond of trust with others is not damaged. Respect is the decision to look inside when communicating to ensure that what we say and how we say it always acknowledges the other's dignity. Respect is sensitivity to others' needs, joys, hurts and sorrows. Respect means playing to the high side of people so they are supported in being all that they can be.

Respect is not something that just happens or that can be demanded of another human being. It cannot be beaten into anyone; it cannot be forced out of anyone. True respect must be earned.

Why in the world would we change the rules for children? I have never understood that. Why would we treat them with less respect than an adult? It seems impossible to me to expect that children respect anyone or learn about respect if they themselves are not treated with respect.

Respect means that there can be no double standard. Right is still right—age has nothing to do with it. What works in the world works in the world. The laws and rules should not change just because of age.

There is a tremendous contradiction if we expect our students to do one thing and we do another. If we demand students be on time with assignments, then we need to be on time with grading papers and providing feedback on their work. If we demand that students put things away, then we need to ensure that our things are put away. If we expect students to keep their word, we must be prepared to keep our word.

The classroom becomes a totally different environment when everyone in it—teacher, aide and students—holds each other in respect.

Don't Pour Ketchup on My White Carpet

Not allowing someone to pour ketchup on my white carpet refers to the level of mutual respect and consideration I want to extend and receive from people.

I want life to work for me and everyone around me. When I say I do not allow others to pour ketchup on my white carpet, I mean I do not allow people to come into my environment or my world and try to destroy it. I leave a lot of space for the people around me to have their world look any way they want, and I expect people to do the same with my world.

This is not always an easy task. How would it look in your world? It may mean not allowing people to criticize the way you have decided to do something. It might mean that students (or adults) are not allowed to belittle others in your presence or that it is not OK for children to punch and hit each other around you.

It could mean a lot of things. Mainly, it means that you take a stand about the way things are going to be in your world and then you do what you need to do to ensure that things are that way.

Be Willing to Lose It All to Have It All

Attachment to the outcomes of situations and to the expected behavior of others gets most of us into a lot of trouble and causes endless hours of heartache.

Most of us grew up in situations where we learned a fair amount of control, and not necessarily the positive kind. We grew up controlling our behavior, controlling our laughter, controlling our anger, attempting to control other people's behavior, or having ours controlled.

This kind of control can strangle the life right out of life. It hinders our ability to relax and enjoy ourselves. We stop smelling the roses or even noticing that the roses are there. We are so involved in the everyday demands, self-imposed and simply imposed, that we lose sight of what life was meant to be.

A healthy amount of control, such as self-discipline, self-motivation and self-actualization, is good. The type of control I am referring to here is unhealthy control. Sometimes we try to control people and situations over which we have no control. We maintain an illusion of the control that we have decided we wanted to have.

THE MEETING

You and I have a meeting scheduled for 8:00 a.m. I decide that I will be there early, at 7:45 a.m. You, on the other hand, have things to do and will be there as agreed. In my need to control, I work myself into a lather because you are not there early and I have decided you should be. I don't have the right to make that decision for you or anyone else.

If my need to control others and life in general is great enough, I might challenge you when you arrive at 7:55 a.m., suggesting that you might have considered getting here early. Of course, this is none of my business, and if you are in your integrity, you might consider telling me so in a nice manner.

Teacher's styles differ greatly. Our need to control the environment in our classrooms varies greatly as well. The important thing here is not that we are turning the classroom over to our students without limits or guidelines, but that we are willing to relinquish our need to control the environment.

Once we implement guidelines, boundaries and groundrules and have some kind of agreement with our students as to what we all feel will work best for our classroom, we as teachers get out of the way and allow it to happen. One of the terms that is often used for this type of agreement is that the students, aides and teachers have all "bought in."

Very often our need to control is the very element that prevents the students from developing their ability to be self-regulating. This relinquishing of control needs to happen just as soon as the students have bought in and are behaving responsibly.

I used to call it the long and short ticket. Once groundrules were laid out and it was clear that they were agreed to and everyone had bought in and understood, students were on their own. As the rules were adhered to, the ticket got longer and longer, with few limits within the parameters. If the rules were broken or not respected, the ticket got shorter and the privileges became fewer. The length of the ticket depended on the behavior of the students, not on whether I could control them or not.

We often control many elements that students could handle independently. If we let students handle these, we can increase their self-esteem and free up our time for more creative thinking. When the majority of our students have bought in and are enjoying their freedom, we can have additional time with students who may not yet be quite so independent.

Administration styles also vary greatly in areas and degrees of control. Teachers, like students, are more likely to contribute 100 percent when they have bought in and then feel free to operate independently, without being controlled by outside forces. In such schools, creativity, excitement, newness, freshness of ideas, parent participation and student achievement appear to be highest.

Relinquishing unhealthy control of individuals and situations is crucial if you truly want life to work. The alternative is coping with continual disappointments, feeling constantly let down by the world in general and the people in it, and losing joy in living. When we are unwilling to allow life to happen as it will, we are in constant struggle with life and everything in it.

Have you ever been river rafting? In river rafting, if you want to get out of the raft and go down the current with your body, you go down on your backside, feet first. If you don't want to get hurt, you hold your arms in, lie back and enjoy the journey. To do anything else is to ask to get hurt. If you grab at the branches or go down head first on your belly, you will get smashed. It's a lot like life—when we learn to stop struggling and enjoy the journey, it can be much easier.

When we are obsessed with having to control our environment and everything in it, we are actually out of control. When we allow things to get to that point, life stops working well. Our level of expectation goes up, our demand level goes up, our stress level goes up. It is an impossible task, like trying to hold the ocean back or trying to keep the moon and sun from rising and setting.

Alternate Plans

Life gets a whole lot simpler when we realize that there is an alternate plan to every situation. So many times we take a position on the way it has to be. An unhealthy need for control takes over, and we sometimes cannot see that there is any other way to proceed. We put our heads down and barrel through an issue, refusing to look to left or right, because this is the way it is supposed to be.

Living that way is very hard. Being around someone who lives that way can be very tiring. Having a teacher who teaches that way is very inhibiting. It is inhibiting because there is no freedom there, no freedom to create or offer feedback, no freedom of movement. In some ways, it is like being in prison.

In the classroom, there are things that need to be accomplished in our lesson plan. These items are important and many times mandatory. However, if you are willing to look at alternate plans, you begin to see that there are hundreds and thousands of ways to get things done. Alternate plans may even allow the students to figure out some of the process themselves. This allows them to experience flexibility and freedom.

Stop! Go Back to Wherever It Was Working and Start Again

We all get off track. Sometimes we can get way down the track before we realize how far off we are. Have you ever been on a diet? Have you ever blown the diet? Usually there are two ways to go after that—go on a total binge and eat everything in sight, or forgive yourself and get right back on it. Perhaps you have gotten to the end of a week and realized that all five days were the same as the week before in spite of your commitment to change the science display, re-do your spelling folders, find three exciting books for storytime, plan some new P.E. activities...need I say more?

You can either be down on yourself all weekend—feel miserable, remind yourself what a bad teacher you are and be too depressed to effect any positive change—or forgive yourself and move on. Every moment is a new moment of now. You can choose to make it different at any time, but you must choose. By next Friday, you can have effected all the changes easily.

Life is the same way. When we run amuck and get off track, the best thing to do is to recognize it, forgive it, go back to where it was working and start again.

Sometimes we look up and cannot figure out how we got so far off target. Do you know the actual definition of *sin?* The word *sin* is an ancient archery term that simply means to miss the mark.

When I realize that I have gotten totally off the track, I try to stop the process and look at where I really am and where I expected or wanted to be at this point. Then I look at where I got off my purpose and decide what I need to do to get back on. The worst thing we can do is to continue when it is evident that things are not working.

Let's say that you embark with your class on a project. It goes along nicely and then for some reason gets off track. When you see that, stop. Acknowledge that the project is off track, and let the class figure out how to get it back on.

Don't forget to have students look at how things went wrong and discuss the options for fixing it. When we assist students to acknowledge the problem and then take responsibility to create a solution, they learn a valuable lesson in self-esteem.

One of the greatest gifts we can give others is to allow them the privilege of figuring out how to get themselves out of whatever they got themselves into. It can be the ultimate learning experience and sometimes terribly difficult for those of us watching.

Here are some suggestions for putting a process back on track.

- Admit there is a problem and stop the process.
- Never blame; forgive if necessary. Blame is *never* positive.
- Identify where the problem may be and when it first began to occur.
- Brainstorm possible solutions.
- Decide on a plan of action.

- Institute the plan and take action.
- Determine checkpoints to avoid getting off track again.
- Acknowledge yourself and others for recognizing the problem and moving toward a solution.

We Do Not All March to the Beat of the Same Drum

It is important that we recognize and give others in our lives room to be who they are while we are being who we are. We might do well to notice that each of us can approach a challenge from a different direction and still create an acceptable result. We can all learn from each other's creative approach to a situation.

The answers may not be in books. Be willing to look around you. A great lesson for your students is to present them with a learning objective. Then ask each student to come up with a way of achieving the objective without duplicating anyone else's way.

Celebrate your differences—and those of your students, their parents, your colleagues and friends. Assist them all to do the same.

Is This How You Want to Spend the Rest of Your Life?

I have challenged you over and over again to look at your life and how you feel about it. Your feelings about yourself and your life are directly related to your own self-esteem.

Now think about this question. *If you had to have in*

your life exactly what you have now for the rest of your life,
would you be happy, fulfilled and delighted with what you
have right now? What would you want to be different? What
would you want to change?

Guess what? You are the only one who can do it. No one,
and I mean no one, can make your life be what you want it to
be but you—not your principal, not your wife, not your
husband, not your children.

If your life is not as you want it to be, you must make the
changes necessary to have it be different. You first have to
decide what you would change. You also need enough con-
fidence in yourself to believe your life could be different. As
soon as you begin to look at your life this way, your own
personal self-esteem will be enhanced.

If Not Now, When?

Where were you ten years ago? What were you doing?
What were your dreams and aspirations? What was your
living situation? Were you happy? Ten years ago seems like
just yesterday, doesn't it? Have you accomplished what you
thought you would in the last ten years? Perhaps you have far
exceeded what you thought you might ever do.

Life is changing faster for us each day then it did in a
month for our great-great-grandparents. We have more
information coming into our lives in a day than they did in six
months. We hear, almost instantly, details from around the
world that they may never have heard in a lifetime. We can
get farther in an hour than they could have traveled in

months—San Francisco to Los Angeles in an hour or San Francisco to New York in two and one-half hours in a supersonic jet.

Think about how far technology has come in the last ten years. Even the computer I am writing this on was not available to me ten years ago. The portable phone on my desk, the telephone answering machine in my office, the VCR on my television—all are recent additions.

How has education changed? What would you like to see in the educational process in the next ten years? Are you willing to take a stand to see that it is there?

If you closed your eyes right now and opened them twenty, thirty or forty years from now, would you have accomplished what you want with your life? After a while in my business, it becomes pretty apparent that people for the most part are not doing with their lives what they want. They have a belief system that tells them they cannot. When you are doing what you want in the way that you want, you provide a shining example to all who know you.

We are capable of so much more. If you are overworked, overstressed and overwhelmed, you might want to consider what you are spending your time doing. When you spend your time doing something you love, something you perceive makes a difference, you get a lot more done in a lot less time and have a lot more energy.

When you spend your time doing something you don't want or like to do or doing something you love in a way that doesn't work for you, it drains your energy—physical, emotional and creative.

Referent Leadership

I first remember hearing the term *referent leadership* in the late 1970s. It was used by a training company to address and define management by example or teaching by example. The term can be applied to all sorts of environments.

What is a leader? A leader is a person who takes responsibility to do what needs to be done when it needs to be done. A leader chooses for the highest good of all when making decisions. A leader gives and receives personal feedback. A great leader has the ability to put ego aside and look at the bigger picture.

Good leaders believe in others and their ability to perform. They also provide an arena for those they lead to test their abilities. Truly great leaders empower people under their direction to be all they can be. Leaders learn from those they lead and are often followers, too. Superior leaders always see their followers as leaders in training. I see teachers as leaders of the greatest measure.

The Pain and the Game Are the Same

What causes us pain and what causes us joy in our lives stem many times from the same things. Our family, our work, our romances, our friendships, our possessions can all cause great joy or great pain. The joy or pain depends a lot on the choices we make in, for and about each situation.

Life is a game, and we each decide how we will play. We choose the rules, the players, the environment. As life evolves, we choose how we will feel about it as we go.

I am who I am today because of all that I have lived through to this point. No matter what lessons I needed to have, no matter how difficult, I teach from my experience and make a difference. What a gift!

As teachers, we can let our students know that even if no one else in the whole world appears to believe in them, we do. We all need to know that someone believes in us in order to believe in ourselves.

I believe that we each have one inherent desire in this life—to know that our existence matters, that when we leave we will leave a mark somewhere. When people don't think they are making a difference and feel they have no importance or value, they become mean, angry and withdrawn. They give up on life, those around them and themselves.

Each of us wants to know that our day counted for something, that we contributed in a positive way to our world. When people believe that, they get excited about each day, because there will be something at the end of it that they can give themselves credit for. Having high self-esteem means knowing that I can be trusted with myself and those around me, knowing that I can and will touch them and allow myself to be touched in a positive way.

Children learn from observing us. They will pick up our language, our behavior patterns, even our facial expressions. They will learn their integrity from us. They will learn as much or more by watching our behavior as by listening to what we say. Winning teachers teach children to be winners!

DON'T MISS THESE OTHER EXCITING SELF-ESTEEM RESOURCES!

Help Children Develop Positive Self-Esteem with These Additional Resources from ETR Associates/Network Publications.

POSITIVE PAMPHLETS

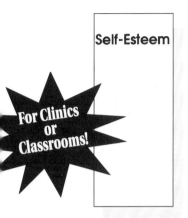

Send for Free Pamphlet Samples!

We provide single copies free of charge for your review. Simply send a stamped (0.29 postage) self-addressed, business-size envelope. Write the titles of the pamphlets on the back of the envelope and mail to ETR Associates/ Network Publications, Sales Department, P.O. Box 1830, Santa Cruz, CA 95061-1830.

Bulk Prices Per Title Begin at 50 Pamphlets for $15.00

READY-TO-TEACH CURRICULA

For Grades 5-8

For Grades 9-12

A PRACTICAL HANDBOOK
For Educators and Care Providers

Into Adolescence:
Enhancing Self-Esteem
84 pages/paper, $19.95

Entering Adulthood: Connecting
Health, Communication and
Self-Esteem
91 pages/paper, $19.95

Smiling at Yourself: Educating
Young Children
About Stress and Self-Esteem
150 pages/paper, $14.95

These are Just a Few of Our Dynamic Self-Esteem Books, Curricula and Pamphlets. For More Information and a Complete Catalog of Over 500 Family Life Resources...

Call Toll-Free 1(800)321-4407
or contact:

Sales Department, ETR Associates/Network Publications
P.O. Box 1830, Santa Cruz, CA 95061-1830 FAX: (408) 438-4284